ON THE SURFACE OF SILENCE

PHOTOGRAPH BY DAVID ANDERMAN

ON THE SURFACE OF SILENCE

The Last Poems of Lea Goldberg

TRANSLATED AND INTRODUCED

by Rachel Tzvia Back

HEBREW UNION COLLEGE PRESS

UNIVERSITY OF PITTSBURGH PRESS

Permission has been granted by the Gnazim Institute, Hebrew Writers' Association for poems on pages 12 and 14, photo of Goldberg, and images from their archive (pp. 5, 139); by Tuvia Ruebner for drawings by Lea Goldberg from his personal collection (pp. 31, 59, 105); and by Sifriat Poalim, for the original Hebrew edition of שִׁירֵי הַיַּחִים © Sifriat Poalim 1971.

Published by Hebrew Union College Press, Cincinnati, OH, 45220,
and the University of Pittsburgh Press, Pittsburgh PA, 15260
Copyright © 2017 Hebrew Union College Press
All rights reserved
Manufactured in the United States of America
Printed on acid-free paper

Set in ITC Legacy Serif by Raphaël Freeman, Renana Typesetting

Cataloging-in-Publication Data is available from the Library of Congress

ISBN 13: 978-0-8229-6490-2

TOWARD MYSELF

The years have made up my face

with memories of loves

and have adorned my hair with light silver threads

making me most beautiful.

In my eyes are reflected

the landscapes.

And paths I have trod

have straightened my stride –

tired and lovely steps.

If you should see me now

you would not recognize your yesterdays –

I am walking toward myself

with a face you searched for in vain

when I was walking toward you.

~ Lea Goldberg

This poem is the final poem in *With this Night* (1964), the last collection Goldberg published in her lifetime.

CONTENTS

Acknowledgments	xi
LEA GOLDBERG: A Short Biography	xiii
TOWARD THE "WHOLE FRAGMENT": An Introduction to Lea Goldberg's Last Poems	xvii
A Note to the Reader	xxxiii

THE POEMS

"A young poet suddenly falls silent"	3
"And the poem I did not write"	7
"In everything there is at least an eighth part"	11

FRAGMENTS

1. "The distance between me and the poem's she"	13
2. "A person rises from his sleep"	15
3. "Just one step"	17
4. "Already the silences are easy"	19
On the Mount of Olives	21
Jerusalem, Earthly and Divine	23
"The clasp of sand and stone"	29
"The day turned"	33
"My entire life summed up in that one moment –"	35
"There were questions"	37
"The face of the waters"	39

SONGS OF SPAIN

    1. Passerby — 41

    2. All Saints' Day in Toledo — 43

    3. On the Road to Granada — 45

    4. With Glory and In Poverty — 47

    5. I Talk to You — 49

A Hike in the Hills — 53

SMALL POEMS

    1. Somewhere in Samaria — 61

    2. At the Small Station — 63

    3. All of Night's Stars — 65

    4. A Yellow Leaf — 67

    5. Another Measure of Distance — 69

"The hills today are like shadows of hills" — 71

"But it was a wondrous spring" — 73

Nightmare — 75

"Yes, I have more" — 79

"Of all your forgotten ones I" — 81

"I'll rise, I will rise" — 83

"The swallows" — 85

Upon Reading Dante — 89

"On tip-toe, carefully" — 95

Also the Fear — 97

On the Dangers of Smoking — 99

"You have no right to pardon in the world" — 101

"We wrote words like"	103
The Remains of Life	107
Illness	119
"The skies have already died. The tree"	121
"For a while now no one is waiting there for me"	123
Answer	125
White Poplar Leaves	127
"Tomorrow I will die"	133
"And this will be the judgment"	135
AFTERWORD ~ by Tuvia Ruebner	141
NOTES	143
BOOKS BY LEA GOLDBERG	151
BOOKS BY RACHEL TZVIA BACK	153

ACKNOWLEDGMENTS

For almost two decades, I have wanted to bring Lea Goldberg's final poems, collected in the Hebrew collection *She'erit HaChayim*, into English. From the first time I read and experienced the singular impact of these extraordinary poems and of the collection as a whole, I hoped and planned for the day I might work on an English edition of this masterpiece. Now, as this book becomes a reality, I am delighted to acknowledge those who have contributed so significantly to the work.

My first and most heart-felt thanks are owed to Tuvia Ruebner, poet and executor of Lea Goldberg's literary estate. It is Ruebner's masterful editing of Goldberg's final poetry texts that brought the collection *She'erit HaChayim* into the world. With fierce attentiveness to and respect for the intentions and incarnations of Goldberg's last poems, Ruebner fashioned a poetry collection of great and abiding significance. I am most grateful also for Ruebner's unwavering support of my work on the collection.

I am deeply grateful to Giddon Ticotsky, scholar of Goldberg's oeuvre and archives, for his critical input and significant contributions throughout this project. Giddon's ever-generous spirit and steady aid have been mainstays of my work on this book; all my thanks fall short of fully expressing my gratitude.

I am wholly and happily indebted to Sonja Rethy, managing editor of HUC Press, for her expert editing work on this collection. Working with Sonja has been an unmitigated joy, start to finish. It is rare to have an editor of such grace, kindness, exacting attention, patience, and intelligence; Sonja has all these attributes, and more.

To David Aaron, director of HUC Press, profound gratitude for his enthusiastic embrace of this project, for his rigorous engagement with my translations and for his invaluable suggestions and challenges that made the work inestimably better. Many thanks to David also for the stunning cover image and design. Above all I am deeply grateful to David for his insistence, through his work and his words, that the art we devote ourselves to in this world matters.

Many thanks to The Toby Press where some of these renderings were first published. Many thanks also to Raphaël Freeman for his elegant design and typesetting.

My deep gratitude is given to Europäisches Übersetzer-Kollegium in Straelen (Germany) and Translation House Looren (Switzerland), for providing me with work havens in which I could complete this book.

Finally, I want to acknowledge my mother, Toby Ticktin Back. Her commitment to and active nurturing of Jewish and Israeli culture, together with her unending passion for literature and for learning, have been a steady and abiding source of inspiration for me. With deep love and admiration, I dedicate my work on this collection to her.

Rachel Tzvia Back
September 2016

LEA GOLDBERG: A SHORT BIOGRAPHY

Lea Goldberg was born in 1911 in Königsberg, East Prussia, and spent her early years in Kovno (now Kaunas), Lithuania. Her mother tongue was Russian and her first poems, written when she was still a young girl, were in Russian. During World War I, her family – like many other Jews – was exiled from Lithuania to Russia, where they wandered from place to place. The arduous and complicated journey back to Lithuania in 1917 was marked by a traumatic and fateful experience for the small Goldberg family: at one of the stops, Goldberg's father was pulled from the train, arrested and tortured.[1] As a result of this random violence, Goldberg's father suffered a debilitating mental illness and was consequently committed to a mental hospital, where he remained, separated from the family. Goldberg's parents were officially divorced in 1931. Her father remained for Goldberg a shadowy figure of absence and the threat of illness.

As a schoolgirl, Goldberg attended the Hebrew Gymnasium in Kovno and soon became fluent in Hebrew (a third language, after Russian and German); it was at the Hebrew Gymnasium where she began writing Hebrew verse and where her first Zionist longings and aspirations found expression. At the age of seventeen she began her university studies in Kovno, and from 1930–1933 she continued these studies at the Universities of Berlin and Bonn (where she earned a doctorate in Semitic studies). Throughout her schooling, Goldberg's teachers and professors recognized in the young scholar a voracious and insightful mind, and predicted that she would have an impressive academic career.

However, with even greater passion and commitment, Goldberg's energies were directed throughout this period to perfecting her Hebrew and to writing

---

This biographic material is adapted from *Lea Goldberg: Selected Poetry and Drama* (New Milford, CT: The Toby Press, 2005), 11–14. All translations from Hebrew are mine.

1. In her autobiographic novel entitled *VeHu HaOr* (*And This is the Light*) – written in third-person – Goldberg describes the event in the following words:

> The border police of the little country. Ignorant farmers in army uniforms focused their gaze on father's yellow shoes. They said that these shoes were an obvious sign that he was a Bolshevik spy. Then they imprisoned him in an empty stable. And every day, for ten days in a row, they took him out – as if they were about to execute him. This game went on for ten days. And the man broke – From then, there was nowhere to go but to the hospital.

See *VeHu HaOr* (Tel Aviv: Sifriat Poalim, 1946), p. 25 [Hebrew].

poems, which were published as early as 1928 in Hebrew journals such as *Pétach*, *Ketuvim* and *Turim*. After a year of waiting for her immigration certificate from the British Mandatory Government of Palestine, Goldberg arrived in Tel Aviv in 1935 (together with the writer Shimon Gens as her fictitious husband); there, the published copy of her first book, *Smoke Rings*, awaited her as a "welcome" surprise, and Lea Goldberg soon took her place among the leading intellectuals and poets of pre-state Israel.

In her Tel Aviv years (1935–1952), Goldberg worked at a variety of jobs, including editor of children's books at Sifriat Poalim publishing house, literary consultant to the Habima Theater, and theater critic for the newspaper *Al HaMishmar*. A few months after she arrived in Israel, Goldberg facilitated her mother's immigration, and the two women lived together until Goldberg's death in 1970. In 1952, Goldberg accepted an offer to become a lecturer in European literature at the Hebrew University of Jerusalem, and moved with her mother to the capital.

As her journals and letters attest, her academic career in Jerusalem was riddled with difficulties and obstacles, "intrigues against me...that the sane mind could not even invent."[2] Despite these difficulties, Goldberg was an extravagantly popular lecturer, with hundreds of students flocking to her lectures, which she delivered in a voice characterized as strange and smoke-filled. In 1960, she helped found the Department of Comparative Literature, which she chaired until her death.

Goldberg was a versatile and prolific writer, with published works that include poetry (ten collections), plays, literary criticism, verse and stories for children, novels, and volumes of translations of European classics into Hebrew (she translated from seven different languages).[3] Her books for children made her a central figure in popular Israeli culture, and generation after generation of children are still raised on her now classic tales *My Friends from Arnon Street* (1943), *A Flat to Let* (1959), *The Absent-Minded Guy from Kefar Azar* (1943), and on the children's verse collected in *What Do the Does Do?* (1949). In the decades since her death, she has enjoyed similar sweeping popularity among adults, with many of her poems being set to music, establishing her work as central in both literary and popular Israeli culture.[4] This significant posthumous recognition, however,

---

2. From a 1956 letter, quoted in Tuvia Ruebner's monograph *Lea Goldberg* (Tel Aviv: Sifriat Poalim, 1980), p. 220n 176 [Hebrew].

3. The range of masterpieces translated by Goldberg into Hebrew includes *War and Peace*, Petrarch's sonnets, the selected poetry of Nelly Sachs, stories by Chekhov, plays by Shakespeare, Molière, Ibsen, Strindberg, and many others.

4. Ruebner opens his monograph on Goldberg with the following anecdote:

does not reflect the marginalization and diminishment *as poet* that Goldberg felt in her life.

Lea Goldberg died of cancer in 1970 at the age of fifty-eight. She was awarded the prestigious Israel Prize posthumously that same year. *She'erit HaChayim* (*The Remains of Life*), her final poems – collected and edited by Hebrew poet Tuvia Ruebner – were published a year later. This retitled collection in its entirety is published here in English for the first time.

On the sixth anniversary of the poet's death, we visited her grave, as we do every year. Her old mother remained standing by the grave. The cab-driver, who had driven her up to the Jerusalem cemetery, turned to her and said: "Don't be sad. What is life? We live and are forgotten. But she is not forgotten. Every day her songs are sung on the radio and the television, and her stories are told, even to the children" (p. 9).

Yehuda Amichai offers the following remembrance of himself: "…as a young soldier in the 1948 war [I carried] one of her little books, much torn and tattered, in my knapsack. […] Her poetry has meant much to me." This anecdote is taken from Amichai's "Foreword" to Robert Friend's translations of Goldberg, in *Leah Goldberg: Selected Poems* (London: The Menard Press, 1976).

Though her work has never fallen out of favor in Israeli culture, the first two decades of the twenty-first century have brought with them a renewed and strengthened attention to her work, with evenings on national TV devoted to her poetry, a one-woman play about her life and work in the commercial theaters, the publishing of her letters, diaries, and archival materials, and the issuing of a two-volume CD collection of her poems set to music, sung by the full spectrum of Israel's performing artists.

TOWARD THE "WHOLE FRAGMENT": AN INTRODUCTION TO LEA GOLDBERG'S LAST POEMS

In 1940, at the age of twenty-nine, Lea Goldberg wrote: "Maybe, just maybe we are learning only now / that the foundation of poetry is *not* / in the formations of harmony, but rather in the great fear / which startles a person's heart before death, with longings for homeland and rest – / always far off?"[1] Of course, Goldberg went on in her illustrious poetic career to construct those aforesaid poetic harmonies, in exquisitely crafted poems with intricate rhymes and rhythms; master craftsperson that she was, her often elaborate verses insisted on forms of harmony and perfection. And yet, the search for poetry's essence remained an open question for Goldberg, her ongoing investigation fully in evidence and unrelenting in the evolution of her poetry. It is only in her last two books – quietly and gradually in *With this Night* (1964), and more dramatically in *The Remains of Life* (1971) – that inherited closed forms with their predetermined rhyme and rhythms were left behind. With these works, Goldberg entered into new poetic terrain, a terrain eventually stripped bare also by the reality of the poet's own impending demise. On the threshold of her actual death, Goldberg revisited the question she had pondered thirty years earlier: Does poetry's truth reside more in aesthetic constructions, or in primal emotion?

This expression of a different poetic truth, a truth manifested in the verses' form as much as in their content, distinguishes Goldberg's final, posthumously published book *The Remains of Life* (*She'erit HaChayim*) – retitled here *On the Surface of Silence* – from all her previous poetry collections.[2] And yet, this is a surprisingly

---

This investigation into Lea Goldberg's last poetry collection is a revised version of an article published in *Nashim: A Journal of Jewish Women's Studies & Gender Issues*, Number 25, Spring 5774/2013, pp. 114–28. An even earlier and much shorter version of this paper was delivered in the opening session of the two-day "International Academic Conference on Lea Goldberg: A Centennial Celebration," Tel Aviv University and The Hebrew University of Jerusalem, held on May 29–30, 2011, organized by Natasha Gordinsky and Giddon Ticotsky.

1. Quoted by A.B. Yoffe as the epigraph to his book *Lea Goldberg: An Appreciation of the Poet and Her Work* (Tel Aviv: Reshafim Books, 1994) [Hebrew]. All translations from Hebrew are mine.
2. Tuvia Ruebner, the editor of the posthumously published final collection, chose the book's title *The Remains of Life* from a poetic series of that name (see pp. 106–117 in this

understudied collection, with very few essays devoted exclusively to it.[3] One can only surmise that this intriguing book, marginalized in Goldberg's oeuvre even as it is commonly recognized as a small masterpiece by all who read it, challenges many of the conceptions readers and researchers have held regarding Goldberg's poetry. In what I see as a purposeful development in her poetics, this collection's predominant use of *fragment poems* sets it apart from her previous work; indeed, Goldberg's final verses as collected in *On the Surface of Silence* are among her most accomplished and daring *because* they are fragments; they make meaning as much from what is not written as from what is written, foregrounding their own inevitable movement into silence. Unadorned, unelaborated, lucid, spare, and precise, the poems in *On the Surface of Silence* achieve, as Hebrew poet Tuvia Ruebner puts it, "the mature simplicity [of] life's essence…a simplicity that no longer needs to prove a thing, not even itself."[4] It is an investigation into the nature and significance of this fragment form in Goldberg's final poems that I will develop here.

The term "fragment" as utilized in literature denotes variously in different contexts; hence one must first clarify the type of fragment Goldberg adopted in these final poems. These are not, of course, ancient fragments like Sappho's, whose material partialness testifies to the eradicating forces of history and whose presence marks always what is unrecoverable, forever lost to time and circumstances. Nor are these the Romantics' fragments, with their conceit of interrupted poetic transcendence, as represented most notably by Samuel Coleridge's dream-vision

---

collection). For this English publication, the collection has been retitled *On the Surface of Silence*, and it will be referred to thus throughout this book. The phrase "on the surface of silence" is from the final line of the third section of "White Poplar Leaves" (see pp. 126-131).
3. While very little research has been devoted to this collection, quite a few reviews of the book appeared upon its publication; Goldberg was, ironically, much in the public eye then, following her untimely death at the age of fifty-eight and the posthumous award of the Israel Prize to her that same year. The reviews, however, focused almost exclusively on the poet's emotional and psychological state while writing these final poems, and little attention was given to the poetic choices and strategies evident in them. One reviewer went so far as to argue that "one must not relate to these poems' poetic attributes in and of themselves," for the poems in the book and the "defining personal process" in the poet's life "are a single unit…inseparable." See Daniel Gedanka, *Haaretz,* Feb. 2, 1971, quoted in Haya Shaham, "On the Reception of the Poetry of Lea Goldberg and Dahlia Ravikovitch by Reviewers of Their Day," in *Sadan – Studies in Hebrew Literature: Selected Chapters in the History of Hebrew Women's Poetry*, II, ed. Ziva Shamir (Tel Aviv: Tel Aviv University Press, 1996), pp. 212-13 [Hebrew].
4. Tuvia Ruebner, *Lea Goldberg: Monograph* (Tel Aviv: Sifriat Poalim, 1980), p. 201 [Hebrew].

of "Kubla Khan." Most importantly, these are not the modernist fragments popularized in the rupture and chaos following World War I, such as those of Ezra Pound and Gertrude Stein, whose rhetorical force resides in their lament of the lost cohesion of a lost world. Goldberg's contemporary fragment is something different altogether. To characterize it, I borrow the term "whole fragment" coined by the American poet and scholar Ann Lauterbach in her intriguing essay "As (It) Is: Toward a Poetics of the Whole Fragment." Lauterbach argues that the whole fragment rejects "totalizing concepts of … unity, closure and completion" and intentionally situates itself on the fault-line between presence and absence, between text and silence. In this liminal space where borders are tested and undone, the whole fragment embraces incompleteness as generative and meaningful. It offers a series of "openings" toward new and multiple "constructions of significance."[5]

Of course, Goldberg did not herself edit this final collection. Shortly after her death, Ruebner, her friend and literary executor, sifted through her notebooks and papers, chose poems, established an order, and added to those retrieved texts the last poems Goldberg had published in journals in her lifetime.[6] With select Goldberg illustrations interspersed between, and in conversation with, the poetic texts, Goldberg's final collection of poems was published in 1971, a year after the poet's death.[7] Obviously, with regard to final authorial intent, the element of the unknown remains, as is unavoidable with any posthumously edited and published book. Ruebner himself raises this question in the brief afterword he included in the Hebrew original: "There's no knowing," he writes, "if Lea Goldberg would have included all these poems [in the collection]."[8] However, this not-knowing does not negate the presence of a clear poetic direction in Goldberg's final writings. The fragment *as form* is already in evidence in some

---

5. Anne Lauterbach, "As (It) Is: Toward a Poetics of the Whole Fragment," in *idem*, *The Night Sky: Writings on the Poetics of Experience* (New York: Viking Press, 2005), pp. 40–45; first published as "On Flaws: Toward a Poetics of the Whole Fragment," *Theory & Event*, 3/1 (1999).
6. After Goldberg's death, Ruebner was appointed literary executor of Goldberg's literary estate by her mother, Tzila Goldberg.
7. In her final years, Goldberg saw drawing as "an escape" from writing and expressed her artistic impulses more and more in the visual medium. See Giddon Ticotsky, *Light Along the Edge of a Cloud: An Introduction to Lea Goldberg's Oeuvre* (Bnei Brak: Hakibbutz Hameuchad/Sifriat Poalim, 2011), pp. 145–46 [Hebrew].
8. Tuvia Ruebner, untitled afterword to *She'erit HaChayim* (Tel Aviv: Sifriat Poalim, 1971). An English translation of Ruebner's afterword appears in this volume on page 141.

of the last poems she chose to publish, and the poems themselves speak with authorial force and certainty.

What engages the reader's eye right from the first poem in *On the Surface of Silence* is the great brevity of the pieces, the sparseness of words in contrast to the abundance of white-page space, and the frequent absence of the traditionally defining – one could say confining – title.[9] All these attributes may be considered markers of the whole fragment. So, too, are the enigmatic, un-contextualized and often unexplained poetic assertions. Here is the collection's opening poem:

מְשׁוֹרֵר צָעִיר מִשְׁתַּתֵּק פִּתְאֹם
מִפַּחַד לוֹמַר אֶת הָאֱמֶת.
מְשׁוֹרֵר זָקֵן מִשְׁתַּתֵּק מִפַּחַד
מֵיטַב הַשִּׁיר
שֶׁהוּא כְּזָבוֹ.

A young poet suddenly falls silent
in fear of telling the truth.
An old poet falls silent fearing
the best in a poem
is its lie.
      (pp. 2-3)

The self-reflexive and forceful *mishtatek* (falls silent) – rhythmically and denotatively more assertive than a simple *shotek* (is silent) – is repeated twice in this tiny five-line poem and announces what will become evident as the collection unfolds: Silence is the leitmotif of this book, as silence is the leitmotif of a poet's life. Silence crouches at the edge of every poem and every page; indeed, one may argue that it is the poet's relationship with silence that sits at the heart of each poem.

Intriguingly, in this epigraphic and enigmatic text, haiku-like in form and sensibility (where meaning is made through the juxtaposition of images, lines devoid of explanatory punctuation), the "old poet" – and Goldberg saw herself as old even from a much younger age – imposes silence on herself for fear that "the

---

9. Of the thirty-eight poems and poetic series in this collection, twenty-five are untitled (which includes the four poems Ruebner grouped under the title "Fragments"). This significant majority of untitled poems is a noteworthy and meaningful deviation in Goldberg's oeuvre, where titled poems are the clear norm. Similarly, two-thirds of the poems in this collection are eight lines or less in length, a brevity that distinguishes them from all of Goldberg's earlier poetry.

best in a poem" is its lie. The phrase "the best in a poem is its lie" (*meitav hashir kezavo*) was written by Andalusian Hebrew poet Moses ibn Ezra (ca. 1055–after 1138), one of the preeminent poets of the Golden Age of medieval Hebrew poetry.[10] On first reading, the "lie" seems to have a negative connotation; however, Ibn Ezra's full assertion casts this poetic "lie" in a different light altogether. "The best in a poem is its lie; and if the poem strips away its lie," continues Ibn Ezra, "it stops being a poem."[11] Thus, for Ibn Ezra and other medieval Hebrew poets, the "lie" – which is the secular poem's artifice, its formal adornments and figurative offerings, which together create a fictional reality of pleasure and erudition – is intrinsic to poetry's essence and *raison d'être*.

However, in contrast to this positive poetic sensibility offered by Ibn Ezra and clearly alluded to by Goldberg in her use of the well-known phrase, Goldberg expresses "fear" of the deceitful "best in the poem" – a fear that results in self-silencing, which, for a poet, may be considered nothing less than self-erasure.[12] What exactly is this deceit for Goldberg, and what are its constitutive elements? The fragment does not offer elaboration or explanation; indeed, in a powerful example of poetic form manifesting poetic content, the poem itself abruptly falls silent at the assertion's end. But considering the classical European tradition

---

10. In his seminal critical work *Secular Poetry and Poetic Theory: Moses ibn Ezra and His Contemporaries*, Hebrew poet Dan Pagis (1930-1986) develops a complex and nuanced reading of the phrase *meitav hashir kezavo* as used by Ibn Ezra and the other medieval Hebrew poets of Spain. Pagis points out that the phrase had, variously, rhetorical, moral, and social significances, dependent to a considerable degree on whether it was referring to the formal "lie" – that is, the ornamental nature of poetry – or the "lie" in content. See Pagis, *Secular Poetry and Poetic Theory* (Jerusalem: Bialik, 1970), pp. 46-50 [Hebrew]. For a discussion of Ibn Ezra, see Peter Cole, *The Dream of the Poem: Hebrew Poetry from Muslim and Christian Spain 950–1492* (Princeton, NJ: Princeton University Press, 2007), pp. 121-22. Cole names Ibn Ezra as one of "the four giants of Hebrew verse in Spain," alongside Shmu'el HaNagid, Shelomo ibn Gabirol and Yehuda HaLevi; see ibid., p. 12. See also in this volume Goldberg's "Songs of Spain," pp. 40-51 where she names herself as "anonymous inheritor" of these medieval Hebrew "princes of song" (*negidei-hashir*).
11. Ibn Ezra makes this full assertion in his Arabic prose work *The Book of Discussion and Remembrance* (*Kitaab al Muhaadara wa-al-Mudhaakara*), a collection described by Cole as "the only contemporary work that critically examines the Andalusian Hebrew poetry in belletristic … fashion" and as "[c]ombining elements of a literary memoir, manual, biography, and meditation on the art of poetry." Cole, *The Dream*, p. 122.
12. Ibn Ezra's *The Book of Discussion and Remembrance* had been translated into Hebrew by Ben Zion Halper and published under the title *Shirat Yisrael* (Leipzig: Abraham Yosef Shtibel, 1924). The phrase "the best in a poem is its lie" was common parlance in Hebrew literary circles following that publication.

from which Goldberg emerged, that of the perfect sonnet and of complex *terza rima* verses, of crafted and complete rhyme schemes and rhythms – a tradition she herself adhered to in much of her life's work – one can reasonably surmise that it is exactly this which Goldberg is now naming the poem's best feature and its lie: aesthetic perfection.[13] Thus, this opening poem in *On the Surface of Silence* may be read as a late-in-life bold statement of poetics, an aesthetic and ethical position that rejects the authority and "absolute" beauty of predetermined forms striving toward formal perfection and completeness, forms which by definition obfuscate the truth of human transience and the lasting reality of human solitude and solitariness.[14]

The "whole fragment," as I read its expression in Goldberg's final collection, foregrounds this human solitude and solitariness. In many of the poems collected in *On the Surface of Silence*, one encounters what American poet George Oppen so exquisitely termed "the shipwreck / of the singular."[15] Certainly,

---

13. In her early poetry collections, Goldberg made extensive use of the sonnet form, the Petrarchan sonnet in particular; she translated Petrarch's sonnets into Hebrew and was clearly influenced by his work. Her best-known sonnet series include "Love Songs from an Ancient Book" and "Love Sonnets (in Thirteen Lines)," in the collection *Al HaPrichah* (*On the Flowering*, 1948), and "The Love of Teresa de Meun" and "Trees" (including the oft-quoted "Pine"), in the collection *Barak BaBoker* (*Lightning in the Morning*, 1955). All of Goldberg's sonnets – including unpublished sonnets discovered in her papers – were collected and published in *Love and Gold Poems: The Sonnets of Lea Goldberg*, ed. Ofra S. Yeglin (Tel Aviv: Sifriat Poalim, 2008) [Hebrew]. Goldberg's most famous use of the challenging *terza rima* form appears in her ambitious nine-part poetic series "On the Flowering," in the eponymous collection *On the Flowering*.
14. "Ideas of perfection and wholeness can easily translate into ideas of moral absolutes," writes Lauterbach, in "Whole Fragment" (above, note 5), p. 43. I see Goldberg's apparent refusal here of aesthetic perfection as intertwined with a refusal of such moral absolutes.
15. Oppen elaborates on this image in his letters: "'The shipwreck of the singular' I wrote. We *cannot* live without the concept of humanity, [that] the end of one's own life is by no means equivalent to the end of the world, we would not bother to live out our lives if it were – And yet we cannot escape this: that we are single. And face, therefore, shipwreck" (italics in the original). *The Selected Letters of George Oppen*, ed. Rachel Blau DuPlessis (Durham: Duke University Press, 1990), pp. 121, 265; quoted by Marjorie Perloff in "The Shipwreck of the Singular: George Oppen's 'Of Being Numerous,'" www.bigbridge.org/BB14/PerloffShipwreck.pdf . With similar poignancy and clear-eyed vision, Oppen writes: "It is difficult now to speak of poetry…. One would have to tell what happens in a life, what choices present themselves, what the world is for us, what happens in time, what thought is in the course of a life and therefore what art is, and the isolation of the actual." Idem, "Of Being Numerous," in *George Oppen: Collected Poems* (NY: New Directions, 1975), p. 168. For Oppen, as for Goldberg in her final book, artistic expression and "the isolation of the actual" are inextricably intertwined.

solitude and solitariness are hardly new themes in Goldberg's poetic oeuvre. From the "alleyways of loneliness" in *Smoke Rings* (1935), her first collection, to the "solitary of the night" in *On the Flowering* (1948) and the great loneliness resounding throughout "The Love of Teresa de Meun" in *Lightning in the Morning* (1955), solitariness and solitude are everywhere in Goldberg's poetry.[16] However, what is new in this final collection is that the poems themselves, their visual and material presence, represent and embody solitariness. Because of their haiku-like brevity, the poems themselves *look* solitary on the page, adrift in a sea of white-page silence. Thus, in the four-page series "Fragments" ("Shevarim"),[17] each small poem-fragment alone negotiates the physical white-page vastness around it as it negotiates the imagistic and emotional vastness expressed within:

רַק מַדְרֵגָה אַחַת.
לֹא תִּפְּלִי לָעֹמֶק.
אֲדָמָה קָשָׁה
לְלֹא חֶסֶד שֶׁל תְּהוֹם
. . . . .

Just one step.
You will not fall into the depths.
Hard earth
with no mercy of the abyss
. . . . .
    (pp. 16–17)

This isolated four-line poem-fragment alone on the page is, I argue, whole; that is, it isn't part of something larger, something else or something lost. This elliptical poetic statement is all there is; there is no more: just one step, and then one more, on relentlessly hard earth. A human existence. There is no redemption; there isn't even the grace or mercy of an abyss in which one may lose oneself (much as the reader may lose herself in the free fall into white space following the

---

16. The phrase "alleyways of loneliness" is taken from the poem "Perhaps" ("Ulai"). With the anaphoric repetition of the word "perhaps," Goldberg's poem recalls the poet Rahel's earlier text "And Perhaps" ("VeUlai"). See *Shirat Rahel* (Tel Aviv: Davar Publishers, 1975), p. 79 [Hebrew].
17. The title of this four-part series was given by Ruebner; in Goldberg's notebooks, the poems were untitled and not arranged as a series. For more on this series, see the endnote on page 144.

poem-fragment, a free fall accentuated by the absent period at line and poem's end). The "mercy of the abyss" is, of course, paradoxical, seemingly oxymoronic; and yet, there is "mercy" in oblivion, in the self-forgetfulness offered by a void.[18] Thus, the real paradox of human existence resides, ironically, in the image of the "hard earth" we must traverse, step after step – in the hard and real fact that our walking across the earth is fleeting and our ultimate return to earth is what endures and lasts. This is the paradox of human existence which knows it is transient and yet pretends it is not; the paradox of the poet who knows she cannot capture the world in words and yet keeps trying.

The acknowledgment of this paradox is part of what unfolds in Goldberg's final book; together with this acknowledgment comes, it seems, an acceptance of final silences. Thus, Goldberg writes:

כְּבָר הַשְּׁתִיקוֹת קַלּוֹת.
הָאוֹר בָּהִיר.
כְּשֶׁאֵין דְּרָכִים
אֵין פַּחַד מִגְּבוּלוֹת.
וְאֵין מַה לְגַלּוֹת
כְּשֶׁאֵין מַה לְהַסְתִּיר.
.....

Already the silences are easy.
The light is bright.
When there are no roads
there's no fear of borders.
And there's nothing to reveal
when there's nothing to hide.
.....
    (pp. 18–19)

One encounters in this poem a surrender and a release; a surrender to silence, a release from fear – perhaps the same fear alluded to in the previous poem, and

---

18. The word *tehom*, "abyss," which may also be rendered as "depths," "deep waters," or "great floods," evokes the pre-creation landscape. See Genesis 1:2: "And the earth was without form and void; and darkness was upon the face of the deep" (*Ha'aretz haytah tohu vavohu vechoshekh al penei tehom*). In this context, the poem may be read as suggesting that the indefinable and ever-changing pre-creation state offered a mercy unavailable in the rigid framework of the post-Genesis world.

the fear evoked in the lines penned by Goldberg in 1940 quoted at this essay's beginning. Now, toward life's end, defenses are down, and the struggle is over. The silence that surrounds this small text also permeates it through poetic statements that end abruptly, are brief, unadorned, bare, and definite. The described landscape has no past or future, no roads toward or from it, and meaning is found in this suspended, singular place of the *now*. Borders are undone and ultimately made meaningless; speech and silence intermingle, as do presence and absence. The tautological equation of the poem's last two lines seems to offer the relief of "breaking cover" (as in the cover of espionage), refigured here as the cover of elaborately crafted form and embellishments, what might be considered the cover of formal authority. What stands in place of that authority is the fragment, offering an opening toward multiple readings (what was revealed; what was hidden?) and toward what might come next.

Not all the poems in *On the Surface of Silence* are as short as the two discussed above; however, even the longer poems manifest the sensibility of the whole fragment. Thus, the thirteen-line poem "The clasp of sand and stone" offers in both form and content this poet's complex self-situating at the threshold between speech and silence, between the crafted poetic artifact and the fragmented, half-articulated saying. A poem of culturally charged images and rich motifs, it reads thus:

סְגוֹר הַחוֹל וְהָאֶבֶן
שֶׁל הָגָר,
שֶׁל אַנְטִיגוֹנָה,
שֶׁלִּי.

סְגוֹר הַחוֹל וְהָאֶבֶן.
הָאַהֲבָה קְמוּצַת הַשְּׂפָתַיִם,
הַגַּאֲוָה הַמֻּשְׁפֶּלֶת,
הָעֶלְבּוֹן הַגֵּא.

בְּדַרְכֵי הַגּוֹלִים
סְגוֹר הַחוֹל וְהָאֶבֶן –
וְשָׁמַיִם קְרוֹבִים –
וּבַשָּׁמַיִם
קוֹצֵי כּוֹכָבִים.

> The clasp of sand and stone
> Hagar's,
> Antigone's,
> mine.
>
> The clasp of sand and stone.
> The tight-lipped love,
> the downcast pride,
> the proud insult.
>
> On the exiles' path
> the clasp of sand and stone –
> the sky nearby –
> and in the sky
> thorned stars.
>   (pp. 28–29)

This poem is surprising on every level, from Goldberg's unexpected affiliation with Hagar and Antigone at its opening, to the "tight-lipped" exile descriptions in its middle, to the sudden transcendence at its end. The two quatrains and closing quintain are composed of telegraphic images delivered in very short, mostly end-stopped lines, in which the syntactic unit is complete and closed at line's end. These poetic choices promote a quiet certainty, and a sense that every moment in the poem, as in life, may be the last. What resounds most forcefully in the poem is the absence of verbs; indeed, there is not a single verb in the thirteen-line text. Verbs in general, and action verbs in particular, are no longer necessary, it seems – and perhaps no longer possible. This is the landscape of the suspended, the unmoving; this is the landscape, again, of no roads and no borders, hence no direction; a landscape of sand and stone and open horizons.

    Certainly the notion of motionless suspension seems paradoxical in a poem about exile: Hagar's exile for being a threat to the single narrative of nationhood; Antigone's, for defying patriarchal law and logic; and the speaker's – from what and why, we do not know. Exiles in general and Jewish exile in particular traditionally connote wandering, endless and relentless movement from place to place. However, the exile here, in a fiercely embracing desert of "sand and stone," is of a different sort altogether. Rewriting the biblical motif of desert as the place one must traverse to get *to* the Promised Land, and rewriting exile as the imposed and punishing state one must endure *away* from that Land, this is a desert and an exile that do not exist in relation to anywhere else; this desert and this exile offer instead an end-to-wandering to or from. The thrice-repeated "clasp of sand and stone" links stanza to stanza and asserts the literal and figurative *hold* of this non-place place.[19] Thus, the traditional construct of exile as not-homeland is revised; indeed, this exile offers an alternative to the very notion of homeland. In Goldberg's poetic and personal trajectory, this seeming embrace and acceptance of the non-homeland is of supreme significance. Having spent a lifetime suffering "the heartache of two homelands," might she be asserting at life and poem's end that in this dividedness one has, finally, no homeland at all?[20] "I left a land not mine / for another, not mine either," wrote Egyptian-French writer Edmond Jabès, describing, perhaps, the emotional reality of many immigrants, Goldberg's too. "I took refuge in a word of ink," he continues, "with the book for space, / and word from nowhere, obscure word of the desert."[21]

Jabès' "word of ink" aspires, it seems, toward stability, offering refuge; however, that stability is complicated by the continuation of the passage, where the once-authoritative poetic "word of ink" becomes a "word from nowhere, obscure word of the desert." Similarly, Goldberg's desert of "sand and stone" is a place both seemingly stable (as in stone) and ever-shifting (as in sand); a landscape of innumerable particles which together fashion the impression of a whole. As I read Goldberg's final poems, this literal desert topos doubles as a trope for poetry's terrain; to return to Lauterbach's terminology, this is a "distilled or stabilized 'reality'" that is, finally, nothing more than "an illusion of syntax."[22] The poem as whole fragment exposes the illusion.

---

19. The thrice-repeated phrase that opens the poem offers us the curious and unconventional word *segor*, which I've translated as "clasp" both to render the denotation of "fastener" and to evoke the sound of something closed/closing (*sagur*), embedded in the Hebrew original. An additional denotation of the word is "pure gold." It also evokes the collocation *segor halev*, the thorax or breastbone, and the expression *kara et segor libo*, "he opened his heart." Thus, in this image of the "clasp of sand and stone" beats the quiet pulse of the human heart.
20. The phrase "the heartache of two homelands" is from Goldberg's oft-quoted and canonic poem "Pine," English version in Rachel Tzvia Back, *Lea Goldberg: Selected Poetry and Drama*, p. 91. Of relevance to this conception of the non-homeland, see Tuvia Ruebner's 2009 *Haaretz* interview where he states the following: "Lea Goldberg wrote that there are [for her] two homelands [the one in which we are born and the one we choose.] I feel that I have two 'no-homelands.' [....] Poetry became my homeland." *Haaretz*, Interview with Dalia Karpel, July 29, 2009. I view the poems of *On the Surface of Silence* as placing Goldberg in agreement with Ruebner's conception of the non-homeland.
21. Edmond Jabès, *A Foreigner Carrying in the Crook of His Arm a Tiny Book*, translated by Rosemarie Waldrop (Middletown, CT: Wesleyan University Press, 1993), p. 79.
22. Lauterbach, "Whole Fragment," (above, note 5), p. 42.

Other "illusions" are similarly exposed in Goldberg's poem. She refuses the traditional paradigm of affiliation and self-identification according to nationality and religion, a paradigm most forcefully present in Israel throughout the years of Goldberg's life. In this refusal, in establishing a gender-based collective identity (with Hagar and Antigone) across ethnic and religious borders, Goldberg exposes the "illusion" of those borders and of the single androcentric narrative of identity formulation. This refusal is an act of feminist "re-vision" – the "re-vision" conceptualized by Adrienne Rich as "the act of looking back, of seeing with fresh eyes, of entering an old text from a new critical direction" and of understanding "the assumptions in which we are drenched."[23] Hence the "old texts" of exile and of what is or is not homeland are entered from a new direction, and the "assumptions" of identity demarcated by national borders and ideologies are foregrounded as the speaker in Goldberg's poem seems to find refuge and, finally, transcendence in the open, indeterminate fluctuation of the unnamed, unbordered desert.[24]

Undoubtedly one may choose to read this place of "sand and stone" differently, not as the refuge Jabès suggests, but rather as a claustrophobic and confining place. I see it otherwise, and I believe the poem's ending fortifies my reading. In the borderlessness of the whole fragment, earth and sky are near each other and eventually merge in the startling and exquisite image of *kotzei kokhavim*. With these thorned stars, or starred thistles, two elements otherwise belonging to opposing and separate realms are linked through the rhyming of their first syllables *kotzei/kokhavim*, thus unifying the heavens and the earth.[25] The image

---

23. Adrienne Rich, "When We Dead Awaken: Writing as Re-Vision," in *idem, On Lies, Secrets, and Silence: Selected Prose 1966–1978* (New York: Norton, 1979), p. 35.
24. Goldberg's refusal to self-identify according to the parameters of nationality recalls her response to the literary debate that raged among the Hebrew poets in Palestine during World War II over the "legitimacy" of writing lyric poetry in wartime. Goldberg was taken to task by Natan Alterman for her failure (or refusal) to write "mobilized poetry" (*shirah meguyeset*) – poems on the horror of war, the importance of nation-building, and the noble sacrifice of young men. Goldberg's response was that poets had the right – even the obligation – to continue writing poems of nature and love, *especially* in wartime. It was the poet's job, she argued, "to remind humankind, every moment and every day, that the opportunity to return and be human is not lost." See Ruebner, *Lea Goldberg* (Tel Aviv: Sifriat Poalim, 1980), pp. 69–74, 116; also see Goldberg's poem *Ha'omnam od yavo'u* ("And will they ever come"), in *idem, On the Flowering* (*Al HaPrichah*; Tel Aviv: Sifriat Poalim, 1948), p. 72; English translation in Back, *Lea Goldberg* (above, note 20), p. 76.
25. I see this merging of heavens and earth as an alternative creation story, a revision of the Genesis creation story in which the world comes into being through distinction and differentiation, through the separation of natural elements from life forces. The

is one of transcendence, of limitless possibility and beauty in the moment, in the singular experience of one's singular place. In his own writing on the desert and exile, Jabès termed this place "the inhabitable infinite," a place/non-place that was for him, and perhaps in the end for Goldberg too, "a haven of grace."[26] The "inhabitable infinite" – or "haven of grace" – operates also on the level of the reader's encounter with the text and her "making of meaning" in a poetic landscape that is regenerative, fluid, multiple and ever-changing.[27]

Inevitably, the sand and star images placed in close juxtaposition in this spare and stripped-down poem evoke God's blessing of Abraham, in which he is promised that his descendants will be "as numerous as the stars of the heaven and the sands of the seashore; and ... will seize the gates of their foes" (Genesis 22:17). This fundamental moment in Jewish national and religious identity formation and the political and ideological framework it proffers are, however, challenged by Goldberg's whole fragment.[28] In place of the promise of a great and numerous nation that will defeat all other nations – a promise based on patriarchy's paradigms of power – Goldberg's sand (of the desert, not the sea) and stars offer nothing but themselves, which is the promise, I believe, of individual moments of meaning and beauty in a fully paradoxical and imperfect world.

The final poem that I will consider offers an additional and elucidating manifestation of the whole fragment. The poem, appearing halfway through the collection, reads as follows:

הֶהָרִים הַיּוֹם כְּצֵל הָרִים
וְהַדְּמָמָה כְּהֵד דְּמָמָה.
הַיּוֹם אֲנִי יוֹצֵאת לַדֶּרֶךְ
וְקוֹל צְעָדַי לֹא נִשְׁמָע.

---

elements in Goldberg's tale reject separation in favor of an intermingling that challenges normative and boundaried definitions and visions.

26. Jabès, *A Foreigner* (above, note 21), p. 7. The seemingly oxymoronic construction of the "inhabitable infinite" bears a strong similarity to Emily Dickinson's "Finite infinity" – a condition or place reached when the "soul [is] admitted to itself," a solitary place of "polar privacy" more extreme than the solitudes offered by space, sea, and even death. See *idem*, *Final Harvest*, edited and introduced by Thomas H. Johnson (Boston, New York, London: Little Brown and Co., 1964), no. 1695, p. 312. Though *sui generis* in nature, Jabès' writings lend themselves easily to comparative poetic analysis, as they are poetic in their precision, in their insistence on isolated images as truth-holders, and in their associative leaps.
27. Lauterbach, "Whole Fragment" (above, note 5), p. 45.
28. The sand and star allusion to Abraham is accentuated by the reference to Hagar, who bore Abraham's son Ishmael and was banished into the desert; see Genesis 21.

הַיּוֹם אֲנִי יוֹצֵאת לַדֶּרֶךְ
וְקוֹל צְעָדַי לֹא נִשְׁמָע

> The hills today are like shadows of hills
> and the silence like an echo of silence.
> Today I set out on my way
> and the sound of my steps is not heard.
>
> Today I set out on my way
> and the sound of my steps is not heard
> (pp. 70–71)

The landscape Goldberg portrays in this six-line poem is, above all, a landscape of uncertainty. The very hills – traditionally viewed as distinct, definite, dominant – are here no more than their own ephemeral shadows, while silence is enigmatically an echo of its soundless self.[29] The figurative language is itself intrinsically equivocal, with the use of simile – a figurative device that proposes a possible similarity between elements (the hills are *like* shadows of hills) – in place of metaphor, which would assert an absolute relationship and complete identification between the two sides of the equation (the hills today *are* shadows of hills). In the Hebrew original, the uncertainty and instability of the imagistic terrain is again accentuated by the lack of verbs in the poem's first two lines. The noun-elements – hills and silence – seem suspended, unanchored in a verbless world. Of course, the missing verbs are only half-missing, in that there is no present tense of "to be" in Hebrew, and so such statements are always verbless. However, the appropriate third-person pronoun (in this case, "they" or "it") often stands in for the missing present tense of "to be," and here its absence is marked.[30] Thus, the opening two lines are balanced on the interstice at their center, an interstice that marks the fragmentary nature of poetic and personal experience as one.[31]

---

29. The aural image of silence echoing itself, or of silence being an echo of silence, is beautifully accentuated in the Hebrew through the doubled *dalet* in *hed demamah*. The aural and visual mirroring of the *dalet* – across the white-space valley between the two words – creates an actual echoing effect. In addition, the Hebrew word for silence – *demamah* – is itself composed of the repeated/echoing *mah* syllable.
30. In my English translation of the first line, I added the present tense of the verb "to be," as the oddity of the line without it far exceeded the effect of absence rendered in the Hebrew original.
31. In an intriguing and oddly relevant reflection on the verb "to be," Lauterbach writes

From within this landscape of uncertainty, into these shadow-hills and echoes-of-silence, Goldberg departs, soundlessly: "Today I set out on my way / and the sound of my steps is not heard."[32] The reader cannot be certain if her footsteps are unheard because they make no sound, or because there is no one to hear them. In either case, the isolation evoked by the image is extreme. And yet, the volitional nature of the speaker's departure, conveyed in the active "I set out" (*ani yotzet*), foregrounds the speaker's independence, even a newly claimed freedom. Indeed, in one of the last two poems Goldberg wrote in her lifetime – the haunting sixteen-line untitled penultimate poem in this collection that opens with the words "Tomorrow I will die" – she utilized a similar image of departure, of setting out on a journey that she claims as wholly her own.[33] "Tomorrow all will be / yours and for you," she writes. "But today I / stand at the threshold / and I'll cross over my border / and none may trespass." In this context, I read the unheard steps in "The hills today…" as an expression of liberation – from frameworks and expectations, poetic and personal, imposed throughout a lifetime.

The poem's assertion of unheard footsteps turns on itself in the closing couplet, which is a word-for-word repetition of the previous two lines, but for a missing period at the end. And so, the unheard footsteps *are* heard, in the echoing final stanza, and the poem's form insists thus on at least one, if not many more, alternative readings to the seemingly categorical nature of the speaker's disappearance into silence. At poem's end, in the white space of the missing period and beyond, the reader can hear the echoing silence of this whole fragment poem. Meaning is made, though it never claims to be more than it is in the moment of meeting between reader and text.

"It is the fragment and the fragmentary state that are enduring and normative conditions," writes art historian William Tronzo. "Conversely," he continues, "it is

---

of the gap between "the reified 'is' of an imaginary yet knowable present and the imperfect or furtive 'is' of the *actual* 'as is.'" *Idem*, "Whole Fragment" (above, note 5), p. 43 (my emphasis). In Hebrew, the "is" is even more imperfect and furtive, as it is in fact a marked absence.

32. The word *kol* in the fourth and sixth lines of the poem, translated here as "the *sound* of my steps," also means "voice," subtly alluding in the silenced sound of footsteps to the poet's silenced voice.

33. Goldberg wrote this poem, together with the poem "And this will be the judgment," in the hospital, in the last days of her life; see Ruebner's "Afterword," p. 141. Both poems make extensive use of repetition, particularly (though not exclusively) anaphoric repetition, giving them a powerful litany-like effect. The many declarative statements in both texts lend them a defiant, assertive tone.

the whole that is ephemeral, the state of wholeness that is transitory."[34] Though "enduring" and "normative," the "fragment" as Tronzo frames it is burdened with negative weight, while the "whole" seems to allude to the solely positive Eden, promised even as ever-unreachable.[35] In contrast, the "whole fragment" as conceptualized by Lauterbach refuses the traditional negative and positive weights of these terms; the whole fragment as manifest in the collection *On the Surface of Silence* deconstructs the duality altogether.

Goldberg's final poems foreground the fleeting nature of artistic creation and the paradoxical nature of writing as ever the present signifier of the absent; however, in that acknowledgment of the absent objects, and of the about-to-be-absent speaker herself, the poems are not mournful. The tone of self-valediction prominent in this final collection conveys acceptance, and even accomplishment. Throughout these fragment poems, it seems that Goldberg is finally at peace with herself, at peace with her poetry and with the approaching end.[36] These stark and stripped-bare poetic texts tell no lies, because there's nothing left to hide; in Ruebner's exquisite phrasing, they have "laid the palms of their hands on the gate leading beyond crafted form, beyond the directing hand, beyond poetry itself."[37] This is the terrain of Goldberg's bold final poems. In this terrain, which had looked so fearsome thirty years before, Goldberg gives us poems of great lucidity and liberation, poems whose visions and truths have the power to keep us company through our own lifetimes, through the reality of our own "shipwreck of the singular."

---

34. William Tronzo, "Introduction," in *The Fragment: An Incomplete History*, ed. William Tronzo (Los Angeles: City Research Institute, 2009), p. 4.

35. Glenn W. Most aptly describes the traditionally negative connotations of the fragment thus: "The very term *fragment* [is endowed] with an emotional tone, connoting loss, injury, and deprivation, that is entirely lacking in such partial synonyms as piece, excerpt, and citation." *Idem*, "On Fragments," in Tronzo, *The Fragment* (above, note 34), p. 14.

36. In asserting that Goldberg's final poems express peacefulness and self-acceptance, I disagree with the standard reading of her work as sad and depressed to the end. See, for example, poet Natan Zach's late review of *The Remains of Life*, in which Zach praises Goldberg's last book as "the most wondrous and moving in her oeuvre" but describes the poems as "without residue of hope, without shadow of amnesty." *Idem*, "'Tomorrow I Will Die': Natan Zach on Poems by Lea Goldberg," in *Hed HaChinukh* (December 2001), p. 35 [Hebrew]. Zach's reading was repeatedly echoed in other reviews which were, in my opinion, profound misreadings of Goldberg's last book.

37. Ruebner, *Lea Goldberg* (above, note 24), p. 202.

A NOTE TO THE READER

This collection *On the Surface of Silence: The Last Poems of Lea Goldberg* strives to provide for the English reader not only the individual final poems of Lea Goldberg as collected in *She'erit HaChayim*, but also the visual and spatial attributes, and hence the reading experience, of the original Hebrew book. As such, the page placement and textual markers of the poems emulate the original as much as possible. One significant attribute of the Hebrew collection not transferred to the English book, however, is its inclusion of thirteen drawings by Goldberg, chosen by the Hebrew artist Aryeh Navon and interspersed among the poems. The bilingual nature of *On the Surface of Silence*, with the doubled weight of text, informed the decision not to include all the original Goldberg images. The desire to render the original's visual openness and spatial quiet was a guiding principle throughout.

Five Goldberg drawings have, nonetheless, been included here in this bilingual edition, in recognition of the importance of visual artistic expression to Goldberg throughout her life and most significantly in her final years. Two of the drawings included here (pp. 5, 139) were among those used in the original *She'erit HaChayim* and three (pp. 31, 59, 105) are from the private collection of Tuvia Ruebner, drawings Lea Goldberg sent him in letters during their twenty-year relationship and correspondence.

The book's endnotes serve several purposes. First, the notes elucidate the biblical and liturgical allusions woven through Goldberg's texts by directing the reader toward the relevant source materials; the second purpose of the notes is to articulate significant aural elements at play in the Hebrew which have been lost or altered in the English. The notes also provide additional historical, biographic, and literary information when such information directly affects the reading of the poem. Finally, any pronounced deviations from the Hebrew original, whether in line and stanza length, or lexis changes, are addressed and explained in the endnotes.

Deviations from the Hebrew poems not addressed in the endnotes are instances of transpositions of words, phrases and/or poetic lines. When I have allowed myself such changes in textual order it has been in order to achieve a desired rhythm or musical effect.

With bilingual editions, the temptation for the reader conversant in the original language is to compare the two texts as though the translation were a mirror image of the original. Of course this is never the case; unlike a mirror image which reflects and inhabits the same space as that which it mirrors, the translated poem resides in a wholly different linguistic and cultural world from the original text. Thus, the verse translator strives toward loyalty and accuracy, even as she recognizes at the outset that the ideas of "loyalty" and "accuracy" are themselves multivalent, changing, always necessitating interpretation. And so, finally, the translated poem stands on its own, an incarnation of "a new music," crafted from losses and limitations intrinsic to the translation process, and from moments of transcendence unexpectedly bestowed at the lexical divide.*

---

* The phrase "a new music" is from Eliot Weinberger's "Anonymous Sources: On Translators and Translation," in *In Translation: Translators on Their Work and What It Means*, ed. Esther Allen and Susan Bernofsky (New York: Columbia University Press, 2013), 24. Weinberger articulates the translator's task thus: "…the primary task of a translator is not merely to get the dictionary meanings right – which is the easiest part – but rather to invent a new music for the text in the translation language, one that is mandated by the original."

For an extended consideration of the verse translator's art and craft, see my essay "Translating the Poetry of Tuvia Ruebner: a Praxis & Poetics of Paradox," in *In the Illuminated Dark: Selected Poems of Tuvia Ruebner* (HUC Press and University of Pittsburgh Press, 2014), xxix–xxxviii.

THE POEMS

מְשׁוֹרֵר צָעִיר מִשְׁתַּתֵּק פִּתְאֹם
מְפַחַד לוֹמַר אֶת הָאֱמֶת.
מְשׁוֹרֵר זָקֵן מִשְׁתַּתֵּק מִפַּחַד
מֵיטַב הַשִּׁיר
שֶׁהוּא כְּזָבוֹ.

A young poet suddenly falls silent

in fear of telling the truth.

An old poet falls silent fearing

the best in a poem

is its lie.

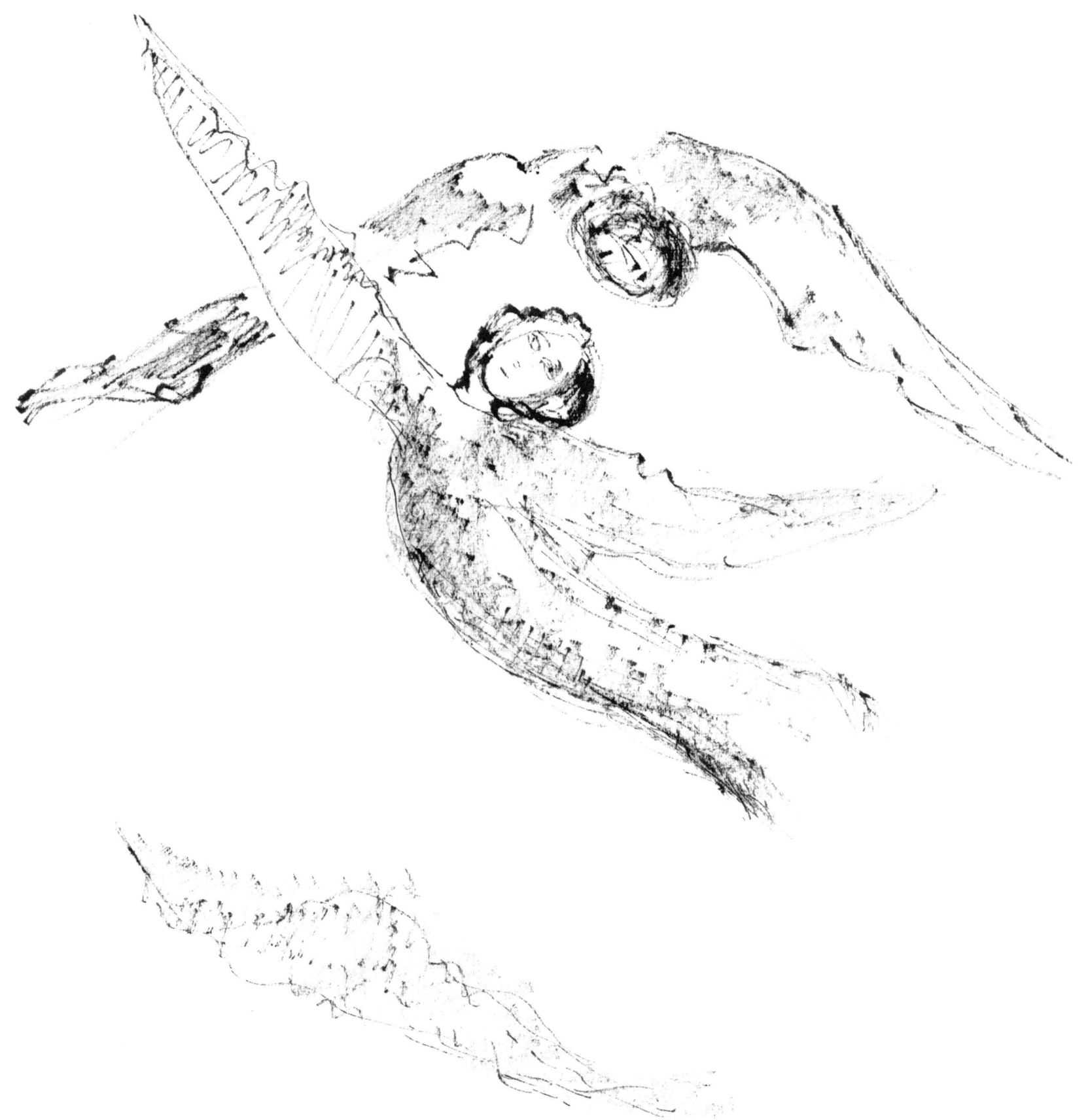

*

וְהַשִּׁיר אֲשֶׁר לֹא כְּתַבְתִּיו
כַּאֲשֶׁר כָּתַבְתִּי שִׁירִים
וַאֲנִי עוֹד זוֹכֶרֶת הַכֹּל
כָּל צְלִיל, כָּל נִיב.
וְלֹא יִכָּתֵב גַּם עַכְשָׁו.

לוּ כְּתַבְתִּיו אָז, הָיָה
אֱמֶת מְעַרְטֶלֶת מִדַּי.
וְאִם אֶכְתְּבֶנּוּ הַיּוֹם
יִהְיֶה שֶׁקֶר גָּמוּר.

בּוֹאִי, רְדִי אֵלַי, בַּת הָאֵלִים,
הַרְכִּינִי עָלַי
אֶת רֹאשֵׁךְ הַמַּלְבִּין.

נְשַׂחֵק בַּמִּלִּים –

*

And the poem I did not write

when I was writing poems

I still remember it all

every phrase, every sound.

It will remain unwritten now too.

Had I written it then, it would

have been too naked a truth.

And were I to write it now

it would be a total lie.

Come, descend to me, O Muse,

rest upon me

your whitening head.

We'll play with the words –

מַה צָּלוּל הָעוֹלָם בַּמִּשְׂחָק הֶחָדָשׁ –

לֹא אָז, לֹא עַכְשָׁו

לֹא אֱמֶת, לֹא כָּזָב

שְׁתֵּי כַּפּוֹת הַמֹּאזְנַיִם עוֹלוֹת וְיוֹרְדוֹת בְּמִקְצָב.

How lucid is the world in this new game –

Not then, not now

not truth, not lies

The two sides of the scales rise and fall

rhythmically.

*

בְּכָל דָּבָר יֵשׁ לְפָחוֹת שְׁמִינִית
שֶׁל מָוֶת. מִשְׁקָלוֹ אֵינוֹ גָּדוֹל.
בְּאֵיזֶה חֵן טָמִיר וְשַׁאֲנָן
נִשָּׂא אוֹתוֹ אֶל כָּל אֲשֶׁר נֵלֵךְ.
בִּקִיצוֹת יָפוֹת, בְּטִיּוּלִים,
בְּשִׂיחַ אוֹהֲבִים, בְּהֶסַּח־דַּעַת
נִשְׁכָּח בְּיַרְכְּתֵי הֱוָיָתֵנוּ
תָּמִיד אִתָּנוּ. וְאֵינוֹ מַכְבִּיד.

*

In everything there is at least an eighth part

that is death. Its weight is not great.

With what secret and carefree grace

we carry it wherever we go.

On lovely awakenings, on hikes,

in lovers' words, in distraction

forgotten at the edges of our being

always with us. And it hardly weighs us down.

שְׁבָרִים

*

הַמֶּרְחָק שֶׁבֵּינִי וּבֵין זוֹ שֶׁבַּשִּׁיר
כַּמֶּרְחָק בֵּין גּוּפִי וְצִלּוֹ עַל הַקִּיר
אַךְ אֲנִי אָמוּת וְהִיא תִּשָּׁאֵר
וְהַיּוֹם לֹא אוּכַל לִסְלוֹחַ לָהּ זֹאת.

. . . . .

FRAGMENTS

*

The distance between me and the poem's she

is like the distance between my body and its shadow

on the wall. But I'll die, she'll remain

and today I cannot forgive her that.

. . . . .

*

אָדָם קָם מִשְּׁנָתוֹ
בְּלִי שִׁיר.
חָכָם שֶׁשָּׁכַח אֶת כֹּל מִשְׁנָתוֹ
תּוֹהֶה וּבוֹהֶה
בִּרְחוֹבוֹת הָעִיר.
אוּלַי מִישֶׁהוּ יִמְצָא אֶת בֵּיתוֹ
אוּלַי מִישֶׁהוּ יַזְכִּיר:
הֲלוֹא רַק לִפְנֵי שָׁנִים אֲחָדוֹת
הָיִיתָ צָעִיר.
. . . . .

*

A person rises from his sleep

poemless.

A sage who forgot all his teachings

wanders dumbfounded

through the city streets.

Maybe someone will find his house

maybe someone will remind him:

It was but a few years ago, was it not,

that you were young.

. . . . .

*

רַק מַדְרֵגָה אַחַת.
לֹא תִּפְּלִי לָעֹמֶק.
אֲדָמָה קָשָׁה
לְלֹא חֶסֶד שֶׁל תְּהוֹם
. . . . .

*

Just one step.

You will not fall into the depths.

Hard earth

with no mercy of the abyss

.....

*

כְּבָר הַשְּׁתִיקוֹת קַלּוֹת.

הָאוֹר בָּהִיר.

כְּשֶׁאֵין דְּרָכִים

אֵין פַּחַד מִגְּבוּלוֹת.

וְאֵין מַה לְגַלּוֹת

כְּשֶׁאֵין מַה לְהַסְתִּיר.

. . . . .

*

Already the silences are easy.

The light is bright.

When there are no roads

there's no fear of borders.

And there's nothing to reveal

when there's nothing to hide.

. . . . .

עַל הַר הַזֵּיתִים

לְנוֹף כָּזֶה אֵין תְּשׁוּבָה
כַּאֲשֶׁר אֲנָשִׁים מִזְדַּקְנִים
עוֹמְדִים בַּדֶּרֶךְ
וְיוֹם קַיִץ חוֹלֵף עַל פְּנֵיהֶם
כְּעַל פְּנֵי אֲבָנִים שְׁבוּרוֹת
בַּמָּקוֹם הַזֶּה.

ON THE MOUNT OF OLIVES

A landscape like this has no answer

when aging people

stand on the road

and a summer day passes them by

as by the broken stones

in this place.

יְרוּשָׁלַיִם שֶׁל מַטָּה וּמַעְלָה

א.

בִּצְעִי אֶת לַחְמֵךְ לִשְׁנַיִם,
יְרוּשָׁלַיִם שֶׁל מַטָּה וּמַעְלָה,
תַּכְשִׁיטֵי דַּרְדַּר עַל הָרַיִךְ
וְשִׁמְשֵׁךְ בֵּין הַחוֹחִים.
מֵאָה מִיתוֹת וְלֹא רַחֲמַיִךְ!
בִּצְעִי אֶת לַחְמֵךְ לִשְׁנַיִם:
הָאֶחָד לְעוֹף הַשָּׁמַיִם
הַשֵּׁנִי
לְמִרְמַס רַגְלַיִם
עַל פָּרָשַׁת דְּרָכִים.

JERUSALEM, EARTHLY AND DIVINE

I.

Break your bread in two,

Jerusalem, earthly and divine,

thorn jewels on your slopes

and your sun among the thistles.

A hundred deaths but not your mercy!

Break your bread in two:

one part for birds of the sky

the other

for feet to trample on

at the crossroads.

ב.

בָּעִיר הַבְּדוּיָה מְהַלְּכִים אֲנָשִׁים.
שָׁמֶיהָ עָבְרוּ כַּצֵּל
וְאִישׁ לֹא חָרַד.
בְּסִמְטַת הַמּוֹרָד
נִתְכַּרְבֵּל עֲבָרָהּ הָרָם.

שָׁרִים יְלָדִים עֲנִיִּים
בְּקוֹלוֹת אֲדִישִׁים:
"דָּוִד מֶלֶךְ יִשְׂרָאֵל
חַי וְקַיָּם."

2.

In the fictitious city people are walking to and fro.

Its sky passed by like a shadow

and no one trembled.

In the alley's descent

its lofty past cloaks itself.

In indifferent voices

poor children sing:

"David, King of Israel

lives on forever."

ג.

מֵעַל לְבֵיתִי
סְנוּנִית מְאַחֶרֶת
כָּל צִפֳּרֵי הַמַּסָּע
כְּבָר חָזְרוּ צָפוֹנָה.

מֵעַל לְעֵינַי
לִפְנוֹת עֶרֶב
בְּעִיר עֲיֵפַת נְדוּדִים
בְּקִרְיַת־עוֹבְרֵי־אֹרַח
חָגוֹת בְּעִגּוּל יֵאוּשִׁים
כְּנָפַיִם
חֲרֵדוֹת וְצָרוֹת.

שְׁמֵי־זְכוּכִית־חֶבְרוֹן.
פָּנָס רִאשׁוֹן שֶׁנִּדְלַק.
סְנוּנִית שֶׁאֵין לָהּ קֵן.
מָעוֹף שֶׁנִּפְסַק.

וּמָה עַכְשָׁו?

3.

Above my home

a belated swallow

all the migrating birds

have already flown north.

Above my eyes

toward evening

in a city weary of wanderings

in the wayfarers' quarter

narrow and trembling

wings

trace circles of despair.

Sky of Hebron-glass.

First lamp that is lit.

A swallow with no nest.

Flight that has stopped.

And now, what?

*

סְגוֹר הַחוֹל וְהָאֶבֶן

שֶׁל הָגָר,

שֶׁל אַנְטִיגוֹנָה,

שֶׁלִּי.

סְגוֹר הַחוֹל וְהָאֶבֶן.

הָאַהֲבָה קְמוּצַת הַשְּׂפָתַיִם,

הַגַּאֲוָה הַמֻּשְׁפֶּלֶת,

הָעֶלְבּוֹן הַגֵּא.

בְּדַרְכֵי הַגּוֹלִים

סְגוֹר הַחוֹל וְהָאֶבֶן –

– וְשָׁמַיִם קְרוֹבִים

וּבַשָּׁמַיִם

קוֹצֵי כּוֹכָבִים.

*

The clasp of sand and stone

Hagar's,

Antigone's,

mine.

The clasp of sand and stone.

The tight-lipped love,

the downcast pride,

the proud insult.

On the exiles' path

the clasp of sand and stone –

the sky nearby –

and in the sky

thorned stars.

*

הַיּוֹם פָּנָה.

כָּךְ לֹא הָיָה תָּמִיד.

הַיּוֹם פָּנָה לִי עֹרֶף

לֵילִי הוּא נֵר תָּמִיד.

עַכְשָׁו יָבוֹאוּ הַשִּׁירִים

בְּלִי חֲנִינָה.

וְלֹא אֵדַע מַה לְהַגִּיד.

אַהֲבָתִי הָאַחֲרוֹנָה.

אֵיפֹה אֲנִי?

וְכָךְ יִהְיֶה

וְכָךְ יִהְיֶה תָּמִיד.

*

The day turned.

It was not always so.

The day turned its back on me –

my night is an eternal flame.

Now the poems will come

mercilessly.

And I won't know what to say.

My last love.

Where am I?

So it will be

and so it will always be.

*

וְכָל חַיַּי סָכְמוּ בָּרֶגַע הָאֶחָד –
קֶרֶן שֶׁל אוֹר עַל קֶרֶן הַצְּבִי.
הָעֲנָפִים שְׁבוּרִים. בַּאֲפֵלַת הַיַּעַר
קֶרֶן הָאוֹר נִרְמְסָה בְּרַגְלִי.

*

My entire life summed up in that one moment –

a beam of light on the deer's antler.

The branches broken. In the forest's gloom

the light-beam is trampled under my foot.

*

הָיוּ שְׁאֵלוֹת

וּתְשׁוּבוֹת בְּסִימַן שְׁאֵלָה.

הָיוּ אֲבָנִים מְשֻׁלּוֹת

לְכָל מִשְׁאָלָה.

אֶרֶץ קִינָה

וְשֶׁמֶשׁ גְּדוֹלָה

וְשִׂמְחָה לְאֵידָהּ בַּלֵּילוֹת

עֵת יָרֵחַ פָּגוּם עָלָה.

*

There were questions

and answers called into question.

There were duplicate stones

for every desire.

Land of lamentation

and large sun

and rejoicing at its sorrow on the nights

when a flawed moon rose.

*

פְּנֵי הַמַּיִם

וְהַמָּאוֹר הַקָּטָן

וְהַדִּבֵּר הָיָה עִם אֱלֹהִים –

וְלָמָּה אֲנַחְנוּ עוֹמְדִים

מוּל הַבַּיִת הַזָּר הַזֶּה

שֶׁתְּרִיסָיו מוּרָדִים?

*

The face of the waters

and the lesser light

and the spoken word was with God –

And why do we stand

before this strange house

with its blinds drawn?

שִׁירֵי סְפָרַד

א. עוֹבֶרֶת־אֹרַח

עוֹבֶרֶת אֹרַח
אַחַת מִנִּי רַבִּים,
יוֹרֶשֶׁת אַלְמוֹנִית
שֶׁל נְגִידֵי־הַשִּׁיר –
שַׁלְהֶבֶת מוֹת־מוֹקֵד
שׂוֹרֶפֶת אֶת עֵינַי,
וַאֲנִי תַּיֶּרֶת.

רַגְלַי נוֹגְעוֹת
בְּאֶבֶן אֶרֶץ נָכְרִיָּה,
וַאֲנִי מְדַפְדֶּפֶת בְּלוּחַ שֵׁמוֹת שׁוֹנִים:

אִבְּן־גְּבִירוֹל
וְגוֹנְגּוֹרָה
וְגַרְסִיָּה לוֹרְקָה.

SONGS OF SPAIN

1. Passerby

A passerby

one of many,

anonymous inheritor

of the Princes of Song –

the stake's deadly flame

burns my eyes,

and I am a tourist.

My feet touch

stone of a foreign land,

and I leaf through a list of varied names:

Ibn-Gabirol

and Góngora

and García Lorca.

ב. חַג כָּל־הַקְּדוֹשִׁים בְּטוֹלֵדוֹ

הוֹלְכִים עִוְרִים וְדוֹפְקִים
בְּמַקְלוֹת לְבָנִים עַל הָאֶבֶן.
יְלָדוֹת פּוֹשְׁטוֹת יָד
בְּבִגְדֵי חַג נְקִיִּים –
וָרֹד וּתְכֵלֶת.

מִגְדָּלִים בַּשָּׁמַיִם
וְחַיֵּי הָאָדָם בָּאָרֶץ.

וַאֲנִי גַּם פֹּה גַּם שָׁם,
חוֹלַת עֹנִי,
חוֹלַת יֹפִי.

2. All Saints' Day in Toledo

The blind walk by tap-tapping

with white canes on the stone.

Girls extend their hands for alms

in clean holiday clothes –

pink and sky-blue.

Towers in the heavens

and human life on earth.

And I am both here and there,

sick with poverty,

sick with beauty.

ג. בַּדֶּרֶךְ לְגְרָנָדָה

עוֹרְבִים בֶּהָרִים
אִלְמִים כֶּהָרִים
וְאֹרֶן הָרִים
שָׁחוֹר
עַל הָרֶכֶס.

אֲדָמָה חַמָּה
וְשָׁמַיִם קָרִים.
עוֹבְרִים הֶהָרִים בְּצֵל צִפֳּרִים
שְׁחוֹרוֹת.

צִפֳּרִים שְׁחוֹרוֹת
אִילָנוֹת שְׁחוֹרִים.
וְאוֹר עַל הָרֶכֶס.

3. On the Road to Granada

Crows in the hills

as mute as the hills

and pine of the hills

black

on the ridge.

Warm earth

and cold skies.

The hills pass by in the shadow of black

birds.

Black birds

black trees.

And light on the ridge.

ד. בִּפְאֵר וּבְעֹנִי

בִּפְאֵר וּבְעֹנִי וּבְשִׁיר צוֹעֲנִים—
וְחוֹמוֹת אֲדָמוֹת וּבָתִּים לְבָנִים
וְהָרִים נְמוֹגִים בַּשָּׁמַיִם.
וּכְלֵי הַנְּחֹשֶׁת כְּדָם בּוֹעֵר.
זוֹרֶמֶת נְחֹשֶׁת כְּדָם בּוֹעֵר.
וּמָגֵן דָּוִד
מִרְמַס רַגְלַיִם.
נְחֹשֶׁת זוֹרֶמֶת כְּדָם בּוֹעֵר.

נְטוּשִׁים שְׁעָרַיִךְ וְאֵין שׁוֹעֵר.
הַיּוֹשֶׁבֶת בֶּעָפָר וּבָאֶבֶן
עֲטוּרַת גַּנִּים,
מְכַנֶּפֶת בַּת־שְׂחוֹק, זְעוּמַת פָּנִים
גְּרָנָדָה.

4. With Glory and In Poverty

With glory and in poverty and with the gypsys' song –

red walls and white homes

and hills dissolving into the sky.

And the bronze vessels like blood ablaze.

Bronze flowing like blood ablaze.

And a Star of David

trampled underfoot.

Bronze flowing like blood ablaze.

Your gates abandoned and no gatekeeper.

She who sits in dust and in stone

garden-embellished,

lifting smiles aloft, glowering

Granada.

ה. אֲנִי דּוֹבֶרֶת אֵלַיִךְ

אֲנִי דּוֹבֶרֶת אֵלַיִךְ הַיּוֹם בִּלְשׁוֹנִי,

גְּרָנָדָה יְפַת הַשֵּׁם,

כְּאִלּוּ עוֹדֵךְ מְבִינָה אֶת נִיבִי הָעִבְרִי,

הֲלֹא תִּזְכְּרִי –

אֶת בָּנַיִךְ הַחוֹרְגִים

אֶת מִקְצָב צַעֲדֵךְ בִּלְשׁוֹנִי –

הֲלֹא תִּזְכְּרִי?

עֲבָרֵךְ מְפַרְפֵּר וְנֶחְנָק בְּשִׁירִי

וּמִי אַתְּ לִי וּמִי לָךְ אֲנִי?

אָנֹכִי רַק רָאִיתִי פֹּה בְּעִבְרִי

פַּרְפַּר לָבָן גָּדוֹל עַל פְּנֵי שַׁעַר הָאלהַמְבְּרָה.

זוֹרֵם דַּם הַנְּחֹשֶׁת וְשׁוֹאֵג כְּאֲרִי

דַּם אֲבוֹתַי בְּמִזְמוֹר עִבְרִי

וְזוֹכְרוֹת אֲבָנַיִךְ פָּרָשׁ נָכְרִי –

5. I Talk to You

I talk to you today in my tongue,

lovely-named Granada,

as though you still know my Hebrew speech,

do you not recollect –

your step-sons

and the rhythm of your gait in my tongue –

do you not recall?

Your past flutters and is smothered in my song

for who are you to me, and to you who am I?

I only saw here as I was passing by

a large white butterfly on the gates of the Alhambra.

The blood of bronze flows and roars like the lion

of my ancestors' blood in a Hebrew hymn

and your stones remembering a foreign horseman –

אֲבָל מִי אַתְּ לִי וּמִי לָךְ אֲנִי?
אָנֹכִי רַק רָאִיתִי פֹּה בְּעָבְרִי
פַּרְפַּר לָבָן גָּדוֹל
עַל פְּנֵי שַׁעַר הָאֱלֹהַמִּבְּרָה.

but who are you to me, and to you who am I?

I only saw here as I was passing by

a large white butterfly

on the gates of the Alhambra.

טִיּוּל בֶּהָרִים

לטוביה ריבנר

א.

עֲלִיָּה אַחֲרוֹנָה בְּהָרֵי עֲרָד.
לֹא זָכַרְתִּי דָּבָר
רַק עֵינַי מָלְאוּ סְתָו.
וּשְׂפָתַי
שֶׁהִשְׁחִירוּ מֵאָכְמָנִית הַיַּעַר
נוֹתְרוּ בְּלִי מִלִּים.
אֲבָל הֶהָרִים
שָׁתְקוּ לִי יָפֶה
מִצַּנַּת הַשָּׁמַיִם
וּמִלֵּב הָאֲגָם.

A HIKE IN THE HILLS

>   for Tuvia Ruebner

I.

Last climb in the copper hills.

I remembered nothing

              just my eyes filled with autumn.

And my lips

blackened by the forest's berries

were left wordless.

But the hills

spoke silence to me beautifully

from the chill of the sky

and from the heart of the lake.

ב.

אוֹהֲבֵינוּ אֵינָם רַבִּים.

בְּעָבְרֵנוּ נִסִּינוּ

לְחַיֵּךְ לְגִזְעֵי אֲרָנִים

וּלְאַבֵּן הָרִים יְרֻקָּה.

וּבְלִי לְחַכּוֹת לִתְשׁוּבָה הָלַכְנוּ

מְאֻשָּׁרִים מְאֹד

עִם כָּל מַה שֶּׁאֵינֶנּוּ שֶׁלָּנוּ,

וְאֵינֶנּוּ אִתָּנוּ

וְאֵינֶנּוּ שׁוֹכֵחַ

כִּי אֵינֶנּוּ זוֹכֵר.

2.

Those who love us are not many.

Passing by we tried

to smile at the pine trees

and at the hills' green stone.

And not waiting for a reply we walked on

so happy

with all that is not ours,

and is not with us

and does not forget

for it does not remember.

ג.

הַשֶּׁלֶג שֶׁלִי הָיָה תְּכֵלֶת

וְשֶׁלְּךָ

יְרַקְרַק.

וּפִסַּת הַשָּׁמַיִם שֶׁלִי –

זְכוּכִית בַּקְבּוּקִים צְהַבְהַבָּה,

וְשֶׁלְּךָ –

קְלָף דָּהוּי שֶׁל פִּיּוּט עַתִּיק.

וּבָאֲגַם שֶׁלְּךָ – פְּסָגוֹת.

וּבַמַּיִם שֶׁלִי – אֳנִיּוֹת.

וַאֲנִי אֶכְתֹּב שִׁיר אֶחָד

וְאַתָּה אַחֵר.

אֲבָל נִשְׁתֹּק בְּיַחַד

אֶת אוֹתָהּ הַדֶּרֶךְ.

3.

My snow was light blue

and yours

pale green.

My parcel of the sky –

yellowish bottle-glass,

and yours –

faded parchment of an ancient prayer.

In your lake – peaks.

In mine – geese.

I will write one poem

and you another.

But we'll be silent together

along the same path.

שִׁירִים קְטַנִּים

א. אֵי בַּזֶּה בְּשׁוֹמְרוֹן

(אֵי בַּזֶּה בְּשׁוֹמְרוֹן קָטַפְתִּי פֶּרַח־בָּר ~ גוגול)

קָטַפְתִּי פֶּרַח־בָּר וְהִשְׁלַכְתִּיו. בַּגֶּשֶׁם
חִכִּיתִי שְׁנֵי יָמִים בְּתַחֲנָה שְׁכוּחָה.

אֵלִי, אַתָּה לֹא תַּאֲמִין בִּי עוֹד! עָבַרְתִּי
כָּל כָּךְ קָרוֹב מִבְּלִי לְהַכִּירְךָ.

SMALL POEMS

1. Somewhere in Samaria

   (*Somewhere in Samaria I picked wildflowers* ~ Gogol)

I picked a wildflower and tossed it away. I waited

in the rain for two days at a forgotten station.

My God, you'll never believe in me again! I passed by

so close without recognizing you.

ב. בַּתַּחֲנָה הַקְּטַנָּה

בַּלַּיְלָה עָבְרוּ הַקְּרוֹנוֹת. לֹא נָשָׂאתִי עֵינַי.
וְכִי מַה כְּבָר אֶרְאֶה לְאוֹר הַנּוּרוֹת הַחוֹפְזוֹת?
צְרִיכָה הָיִיתִי לָדַעַת מֵרֹאשׁ: הָרַכֶּבֶת הַזֹּאת
אֵינָהּ נֶעֱצֶרֶת בַּתַּחֲנָה הַקְּטַנָּה.

2. At the Small Station

At night the boxcars passed by. I didn't lift up my eyes.

For what could I possibly see in the glow of their fleeting light?

I should have already known: this train

doesn't stop at the small station.

ג. כָּל כּוֹכְבֵי הַלֵּיל

כָּל כּוֹכְבֵי הַלַּיְלָה הַגְּדוֹלִים נוֹתְרוּ שָׁם.
הַשָּׁמַיִם שָׁמַיִם לֵאלֹהִים.
הַחֲרָטוֹת שֶׁלִּי אֵינָן יָפוֹת.
הָעֲנָנִים שֶׁלִּי נְמוּכִים.

3. All of Night's Stars

All of night's large stars abide there.

The heavens are the heavens of the Lord.

My regrets are not beautiful.

My clouds are low.

ד. עָלֶה צָהֹב

אֲנִי לֹא בַּמִּדְבָּר. פֹּה יֵשׁ שָׁעוֹן
וַאֲנִי מְפַחֶדֶת לָבוֹא בְּאִחוּר.
פֹּה הָרוּחַ נוֹשֵׂא עָלֶה צָהֹב
וּמֵבִיא אוֹתוֹ עַד פֶּתַח בֵּיתִי.
אֲנִי לֹא בַּמִּדְבָּר.

4. A Yellow Leaf

I am not in the desert. Here there's a clock

and I'm afraid of arriving late.

Here the wind carries a yellow leaf

and brings it to my doorstep.

I am not in the desert.

ה. עוֹד כִּבְרַת דֶּרֶךְ

עוֹד כִּבְרַת דֶּרֶךְ. עוֹד מָחָר וְעוֹד מָחָר.
וּמָה אָמַר אָז? וּלְמִי אָמַר?
וְאֵיךְ אֶתֵּן הַדִּין וְלֹא נוֹתְרוּ עֵדִים?
אֲנִי הָיִיתִי שַׁעַר עַל הַגְּבוּל,
שֶׁבּוֹ עָמְדוּ הַנִּפְרָדִים.

5. Another Measure of Distance

Another measure of distance. Another tomorrow and another.

What will I say then? And to whom?

And how will I render judgment when no witnesses remain?

I was a gate on the border

where the leave-takers stood.

*

הֶהָרִים הַיּוֹם כְּצֵל הָרִים

וְהַדְּמָמָה כְּהֵד דְּמָמָה.

הַיּוֹם אֲנִי יוֹצֵאת לַדֶּרֶךְ

וְקוֹל צְעָדַי לֹא נִשְׁמָע.

הַיּוֹם אֲנִי יוֹצֵאת לַדֶּרֶךְ

וְקוֹל צְעָדַי לֹא נִשְׁמָע

*

The hills today are like shadows of hills

and the silence like an echo of silence.

Today I set out on my way

and the sound of my steps is not heard.

Today I set out on my way

and the sound of my steps is not heard

*

אֲבָל הֲרֵי הָיָה אָבִיב מֻפְלָא

דְּגֵי כֶּסֶף קְטַנִּים צָלְלוּ בְּעֵינֶיךָ

וּדְמוּת עֵינְךָ בְּעֵינַי צָלְלָה

וְיָכֹלְנוּ לִשְׁקֹעַ: מְצוּלָה בִּמְצוּלָה –

דְּגֵי כֶּסֶף קְטַנִּים נֶעֶלְמוּ מֵעֵינֶיךָ.

*

But it was a wondrous spring

tiny silver fish swam in your eyes

and the image of your eyes swam in my eyes

and we could sink: fathom after fathom –

the tiny silver fish have disappeared from your eyes.

סִיוּט

וְעֵת נִגְזַר עָלַי לֹא לַחֲכּוֹת
כִּמְעַט אֲשֶׁר הִצְלַחְתִּי גַּם לִשְׁכּוֹחַ.
לִמְנוֹת שָׁעוֹת רֵיקוֹת, אֲרֻכּוֹת
בְּאֵין תִּקְוָה שֶׁלַּמַּרְגּוֹעַ –
וְאֵיךְ אֵדַע אִם זֹאת הִיא הַלְּבָנָה?
הָעֵר אוֹתִי, אֵינֶנִּי יְשֵׁנָה.

מָחָר? אַךְ גַּם אֶתְמוֹל הָיָה מָחָר.
אִישׁ לֹא בִּקֵּשׁ, וְכָךְ נִקְבַּע הַשֶּׁקֶט.
רַק מִמֶּרְחָק שָׁמַעְתִּי קוֹל נִחָר –
וַדַּאי דַּלְתָּם שֶׁל הַשְּׁכֵנִים חוֹרֶקֶת.
וְכָךְ הַיּוֹם. פִּתְאֹם חָלְפָה שָׁנָה.
הָעֵר אוֹתִי, אֵינֶנִּי יְשֵׁנָה.

כִּמְעַט לִשְׁכּוֹחַ. רַק שָׁעָה אַחַת

NIGHTMARE

And the moment it was decreed I shouldn't wait

I almost managed also to forget.

To count empty, endless hours

without hope that comes in rest –

and how will I know if this is the moon?

Wake me, I'm not asleep.

Tomorrow? But yesterday was a tomorrow too.

No one asked, and thus silence was set.

Only from a distance I heard a parched sound –

doubtlessly the neighbors' door creaking.

And so it is today. Suddenly a year has passed.

Wake me, I'm not asleep.

Almost to forget. Only one hour

מְשָׁעוֹת הַיּוֹם תָּמִיד אוֹתִי חוֹנֶקֶת.

גָּרוֹן חָצוּי, כְּעוֹף אֲשֶׁר נִשְׁחַט.

הִנֵּה נָפַל. וְשׁוּב נִקְבַּע הַשֶּׁקֶט.

הַכֹּל צָפוּי. אֱמֶת וֶאֱמוּנָה.

הָעֵר אוֹתִי. אֵינֶנִּי יְשֵׁנָה.

from the day's hours always chokes me.

Slit throat, like a slaughtered chicken.

Here it fell. And again silence is set.

Everything is foretold. Truth and faith.

Wake me. I'm not asleep.

*

כֵּן, יֵשׁ לִי עוֹד

עוֹד יוֹתֵר יָפוֹת,

עוֹד יוֹתֵר יְקָרוֹת,

יֵשׁ לִי עוֹד:

מִלִּים שֶׁל עִטּוּר

וְחָכְמָה

וּמוֹתָרוֹת

וּמִלִּים שֶׁל אֱמֶת.

אִלְמָלֵא הַכְּנִיעָה

וְהַדַּעַת

הַשְּׁלֵמָה

הָיִיתִי עוֹרֶכֶת אוֹתָן לְפָנֶיךָ

כְּמַחֲרֹזֶת אִיִּים קְסוּמָה.

*

Yes, I have more

more beautiful still,

more precious still,

I have more:

words of adornment

and wisdom

and extravagance

and words of truth.

Were it not for the surrender

and the perfect

knowledge

I would set them before you

like an enchanted necklace of islands.

*

מִכָּל נִשְׁכָּחֶיךָ אֲנִי
הַשְּׁכוּחָה בְּיוֹתֵר.
מִכָּל הַפָּנִים
שֶׁרָאִיתָ בָּרְאִי
פָּנַי
הַשְּׁקוּפִים בְּיוֹתֵר.
וְקוֹלִי
נָמוּךְ מִשֶּׁלֶּךְ. וּשְׁמִי
חָרוּט עַל אֶבֶן כְּבֵדָה
בְּתַחְתִּית הַבְּאֵר.

*

Of all your forgotten ones I

am the most forgotten.

Of all the faces

you have seen in the mirror

my face

is the most transparent.

And my voice

is lower than a cut field. And my name

is engraved on a heavy stone

at the bottom of the well.

*

אָקוּם, אֲנִי אָקוּם

מִשְּׁנָתִי

בְּרוּחַ אַחֶרֶת,

בְּאֶרֶץ אַחֶרֶת

שֶׁאֵין בָּהּ אַהֲבָה.

צִפֳּרֵי הַטַּל הַזּוֹהֲרוֹת

עַל הַתַּיִל

יָדַעְתִּי, שָׁכַחְתִּי.

אֲנִי שָׁכַחְתִּי.

אֲנִי אַחֶרֶת.

אֲנִי אַחֶרֶת.

אֲנִי חָפְשִׁית.

אֲנִי חָפְשִׁית כְּסִילוֹן הַמַּיִם,

רַעֲנַנָּה וְלֹא אֶזְדַּקֵּן,

לֹא אֶזְדַּקֵּן, חָיִיתִי אֵין־סוֹף

מֵאָה שָׁנָה וְלַיְלָה אֶחָד.

*

I'll rise, I will rise

from my sleep

in a different spirit,

in a different land

where there is no love.

The shining morning birds

on the barbed fences

I knew, I've forgotten.

I have forgotten.

I am other.

I am other.

I am free.

I am as free as the water torrent,

fresh and I'll never grow old,

never growing old, I lived on endlessly

a hundred years and one night.

*

הַסְנוּנִיּוֹת

הִרְחִיקוּ עוּף –

אֲבָל חָזְרוּ אֵלַי.

הָעֲנָנִים

הִרְחִיקוּ נְדוֹד,

חָשַׁבְתִּי, לִבְלִי שׁוּב –

אֲבָל חָזְרוּ אֵלַי.

וְהַדְּמָמָה הָיְתָה שְׁלֵמָה

לַעֲיֵפָה.

מֵעֵבֶר לַחוֹמָה

כִּמְעַט לֹא נִשְׁקְפָה

הָעִיר הָעַתִּיקָה וְהַיָּפָה.

וְרַק אֶחָד

*

The swallows

flew far off –

but they came back to me.

The clouds

wandered far away,

not to return, I thought –

but they came back to me.

The silence was overwhelmingly

complete.

Beyond the wall

almost unseen

the beautiful and old city.

And only one

אֲשֶׁר הָיָה קָרוֹב
וְלֹא חָזַר אֵלַי.

וְהוּא כָּלוּא
עַד עוֹלָם
בְּתוֹךְ שִׁירַי.

who was close

and never came back to me.

He is imprisoned

forever

in my poems.

עִם קְרִיאַת דַּנְטֶה

non piu leggemmo avanti (Canto V)

א.

בּוֹא, אֵפוֹא, וְנֵשֵׁב וּנְדַפְדֵּף

בַּסֵּפֶר הַיָּשָׁן.

שָׁעָה מִשָּׁעוֹת לִפְנֵי הַצָּהֳרַיִם.

כָּל הַשָּׁמַיִם

נוֹתְרוּ בַּחוּץ עִם קַיִץ מְלַהֵט.

וּפֹה בַּחֶדֶר רַק אֲנַחְנוּ –

עִם סֵפֶר שֶׁקְּרָאנוּ

וְשָׁכַחְנוּ.

ברקע השיר אהבת פרנציסקה די רימיני לגיסה פאולו כמתוארת בשיר החמישי שב"תפת". אהבה אסורה זו ניצתה כאשר "לענג-לב קראנו על לנצלוט, איך השיאו האהב... אך דף אחד פִּתָּנוּ וניצחנו... וזה שלא נפרד לעד ממני כלו רוטט נשק את פי בפיהו" (תרגום: עמנואל אולסבנגר).

UPON READING DANTE

non piu leggemmo avanti (Canto V)

1.

Come, then, we'll sit and browse

through the old book.

An hour of the pre-afternoon hours.

The entire sky

remains outside with the scorching summer.

And here in the room, just us –

with a book we had read

and forgotten.

The backdrop to this poem is the love of Francesca da Rimini for her brother-in-law Paolo as described in Canto V of *The Inferno*. This forbidden love was sparked when "…we read of Lancelot – how love had overcome him.… yet one point alone defeated us … and this one, who never shall be parted from me, while all his body trembled, kissed my mouth" (Translation by Allen Mandelbaum).

e caddi come corpo morto cadi

ב.

"נָפַלְתִּי כִּגְוִיָּה מֵתָה נוֹפֶלֶת" –
בְּרַחֲמִי
נַפְשִׁי שֶׁלִּי בַּתֹּפֶת
אֲשֶׁר בְּסִכְלוּתִי וּלְתֻמִּי
בְּמוֹ יָדַי בָּנִיתִי לְעַצְמִי.

השיר מסתיים בדברי דנטה עצמו: "ובכיותיו את רחמי העירו. ואתעלף כפשע מן המות, נופל כמו גופה מתה נופלת" (תרגום: עמנואל אולסבנגר).

e caddi come corpo morto cade

2.

"I fell as a dead body falls" –

in my pity

my very own soul in the inferno

which with my folly and naïveté

I had built with my own hands for me.

Canto V ends with the words of Dante himself: "And while one spirit said these words to me, the other wept, so that – because of pity – I fainted, as if I had met my death. And then I fell as a dead body falls" (translated by Allen Mandelbaum).

ג.

בְּחַיֵּיהֶם וּבְמוֹתָם לֹא נִפְרָדוּ.

וְזֶה הָיָה חֲזוֹן הַגֵּיהִנּוֹם.

עֶרֶב.

הָאָרֶץ נוֹשֶׁמֶת אֲדֵי נְשִׁימַת שָׁמֶיהָ.

וַאֲנִי לְבַדִּי.

3.

In their lives and in their deaths they were not divided.

That was hell's prophecy.

Evening.

The land is breathing vapors of its sky's breath.

And I am alone.

*

עַל בְּהוֹנוֹת רַגְלַיִם, בִּזְהִירוּת
לָלֶכֶת מִסָּבִיב לְשַׁלְוֲתְכֶם,
לִשְׁמוֹר עַל הַחִיּוּךְ, פֶּן יִתְעַקֵּם
מַרְאֵה פָּנַי בְּזֹהַר אִישׁוֹנְכֶם.

כָּךְ עַד הַסּוֹף. וְגַם עַל סַף קִבְרִי
אֶת פִּי יִרְצֶה לִצְעוֹק וְיִפָּתַח
יֹאמַר לִי מִישֶׁהוּ: הִזָּהֲרִי,
הַיְלָדִים יוּכְלוּ לִרְאוֹת אוֹתָךְ!

*

On tip-toe, carefully

skirting your tranquility,

preserving the smile, lest my face become

crooked in your pupils' radiance.

Thus till the end. And even at my grave's edge

when my mouth, wanting to shout, will open

Someone will tell me: Take care,

the children will notice!

גַּם הַפַּחַד

הַלֵּילוֹת שֶׁהָיוּ בּוֹרוֹת שְׁחוֹרִים
שְׁקוּפִים עַכְשָׁו.
הַפְּחָדִים שֶׁהָלְכוּ עַל כַּפּוֹת עַכְבָּרִים
אֵינָם מַפְחִידִים עַכְשָׁו
וְהַמָּוֶת אֲשֶׁר כְּבָר יָשַׁב בִּגְרוֹנֵךְ –
אֲבָל אַתְּ חַיָּה עַכְשָׁו.
גַּם לְאֵלֶּה שֶׁלֹּא בָּכוּ כָּמוֹךְ
עֵינַיִם דֵּהוֹת עַכְשָׁו.

גַּם לְאֵלֶּה שֶׁלֹּא צָעֲקוּ כָּמוֹךְ
קוֹלוֹת חֲלוּדִים עַכְשָׁו.
אִם הָאֹשֶׁר חָלַף – דַּרְכּוֹ לַחֲלֹף
וְאֵין מַסְפִּידִים עַכְשָׁו.
אֲבָל הַפַּחַד –
נוֹרָא לְהוֹדוֹת –
גַּם הַפַּחַד הָיָה לַשָּׁוְא!

ALSO THE FEAR

The nights that were black pits

are translucent now.

The fears that walked on mouse paws

are not fearsome now

and the death that already sat in your throat –

but you are alive now.

Also those who didn't cry like you

their eyes are dim now.

Also those who didn't shout like you

their voices are rusty now.

If happiness has vanished – its fashion is to vanish

and there's no eulogizing now.

But the fear –

it's terrible to admit –

also the fear was in vain!

עַל הַנֶּזֶק שֶׁבָּעָשָׁן

בֹּקֶר גָּשׁוּם. לֹא לָקוּם. לֹא לְעַשֵּׁן, אֲפִלּוּ
לֹא לְהַרְבּוֹת בִּקְרִיאָה. אֵיזֶה אָבִיב מְשֻׁנֶּה!
אֵיזֶה אָבִיב מְשֻׁנֶּה. חֹשֶׁךְ בַּבֹּקֶר כְּאִלּוּ...
לֹא לְהַרְבּוֹת בִּקְרִיאָה. אֵיזֶה אָבִיב מִתְעַנֵּן!

פַּעַם הָיִית מִתְאוֹנֶנֶת. עָזַר לָךְ? הֶחֱיָה אֶת מֵתַיִךְ?
הַכְּאֵב שֶׁבַּגּוּף, שֶׁבַּשִּׁיר, בָּעִתּוֹן. בְּשִׁיר הַשִּׁירִים.
סָיִג לַחָכְמָה? יִתָּכֵן. טוֹב שֶׁלָּמַדְנוּ בֵּינְתַיִם
לֹא לְהָעִיר שְׁכֵנִים, לֹא לְהַטְרִיד חֲבֵרִים.

בֹּקֶר גָּשׁוּם. לֹא לָקוּם. לַיְלָה עָבַר בְּשֶׁקֶט.
לַיְלָה עָבַר. וְעַכְשָׁו – אֵיזֶה אָבִיב מִתְעַנֵּן.
בֹּקֶר כְּמוֹ לַיְלָה. זֶה טוֹב. רַק הַדְּמָמָה חוֹנֶקֶת.
אֵיזֶה אָבִיב כָּבֵד! אָמַרְתִּי לָךְ: לֹא לְעַשֵּׁן.

ON THE DANGERS OF SMOKING

A rainy morning. Don't get up. Don't smoke, don't

even read too much. What a strange spring!

What a strange spring. As though a darkness in morning…

Don't read too much. What a beclouded spring!

You used to complain. Did it help? Did it bring back your dead?

The pain of the body, of the song, of the newspaper. Of the Song of Songs.

Silence the fence around wisdom? Perhaps. Lucky we've learned since

not to wake neighbors, or bother friends.

A rainy morning. Don't get up. Night passed quietly.

Night passed. And now – what a beclouded spring!

A morning like night. That's good. Only the silence stifles.

What a heavy spring! I told you: Don't smoke.

*

אֵין לָךְ זְכוּת חֲנִינָה בָּעוֹלָם.
הַכֹּל הָכְרַע.
חֲלוֹמוֹתַיִךְ טוֹבְעִים בַּיָּם
וְאַתְּ אוֹמֶרֶת שִׁירָה.

*

You have no right to pardon in the world.

All has been determined.

Your dreams drown in the sea

and you speak poetry.

*

אֲנַחְנוּ כָּתַבְנוּ מִלִּים כְּגוֹן:
אַהֲבָה, אַכְזָבָה, וְשִׂמְחָה וְיָגוֹן,
וְהֵן דָּנוּ אוֹתָנוּ בְּדִין אֱמֶת.
בָּרוּךְ דַּיַּן אֱמֶת.

וַאֲנַחְנוּ כָּתַבְנוּ מִלִּים אֲחֵרוֹת:
חֲלָלִים וְקוֹטְלִים וּפְרָעוֹת וּגְזֵרוֹת,
וְהֵן דָּנוּ אוֹתָנוּ בְּדִין אֱמֶת.
בָּרוּךְ דַּיַּן אֱמֶת.

. . . . .

*

We wrote words like:

Love, Disappointment, Happiness and Grief,

and they judged us by a Truthful Judgment.

Blessed is the True Judge.

And we wrote words like:

Slayers and Slain, Riots and Decrees,

and they judged us by a Truthful Judgment.

Baruch dayan emet.

· · · · ·

שְׁאֵרִית הַחַיִּים

א.

הָלַכְתִּי אֶל הַלַּיְלָה הַזֶּה
שֶׁאֵינֶנּוּ נִגְמָר
וּפִתְאֹם הָיָה בֹּקֶר
וְהַשֶּׁמֶשׁ הֵאִירָה
אֶת פְּנֵי הַחַיִּים
שֶׁקִּנְאוּ בַּמֵּתִים.

THE REMAINS OF LIFE

I.

I strode into this night

which is endless

and suddenly it was morning

and the sun lit up

the faces of the living

who envied the dead.

ב.

"שְׁאֵרִית הַחַיִּים" כָּךְ אָמַר,

"שְׁאֵרִית הַחַיִּים הִיא תְּבוּנָה אוֹ סִכְלוּת

וְלָד הַבְּרֵרָה."

2.

"The remains of life," so he said,

"the remains of life are wisdom or folly

and the choice is yours."

ג.

עֶשֶׂר פְּעָמִים
וְאוּלַי עֶשְׂרִים
עָבַרְתִּי בַּמָּקוֹם הַזֶּה
בְּשָׁלוֹם.
אֲבָל מִי עָרֵב
שֶׁהַיּוֹם אֶעֱבֹר
בַּמָּקוֹם הַזֶּה
בְּשָׁלוֹם.

3.

Ten times

and maybe twenty

I passed by this place

in peace.

But who's to say

that today I'll pass

by this place

in peace.

ד.

שֶׁלֶג יָרַד

וּבְאֶרֶץ זָרָה

הָיְתָה מִלְחָמָה

וְהֵם מֵתוּ בַּשֶּׁלֶג

(כְּמוֹ פֹּה בָּאָבִיב)

בְּאֶרֶץ זָרָה.

4.

Snow fell

and in a foreign land

there was a war

and they died in the snow

(as they do here in the spring)

in a foreign land.

ה.

הָיִינוּ צְעִירִים מְאֹד

וַעֲנִיִּים מְאֹד

וְחַיֵּינוּ טְלָאִים

וְקָרָאנוּ סְפָרִים

וּבָעֶרֶב הָלַכְנוּ לִרְקוֹד –

לִפְעָמִים הָיִינוּ גַם

מְאֻשָּׁרִים.

5.

We were very young

and very poor

and our lives were a patchwork

and we read books

and in the evening we went dancing –

sometimes we were also

happy.

ו.

הָיִינוּ צְעִירִים בְּלִי תִּקְוָה
בָּגַרְנוּ בְּלִי אֱמוּנָה
מַזְקִינִים בְּלִי טְעָנוֹת.

6.

We were young without hope

we grew up without faith

we grow old without complaint.

מַחֲלָה

הָעוֹלָם עוֹד עוֹמֵד בְּעֵינוֹ

וְעוֹמֵד בְּעֵינִי.

מַשֶּׁהוּ

הִדְבִּיק עַל שְׁמֻשַּׁת חַלּוֹנִי

פִּסַּת שָׁמַיִם

וּתְרִיסוֹ שֶׁל שְׁכֵנִי.

רַק בַּלַּיְלָה

עוֹמֵד הָעוֹלָם לְבַדּוֹ בְּעֵינוֹ,

וַאֲנִי

הוֹלֶכֶת מִמֶּנּוּ

עַל פְּנֵי תְּהוֹם זִכְרוֹנִי.

ILLNESS

The world still stands its ground

and stands my ground.

Someone

has pasted on my window pane

a piece of the sky

and my neighbor's blinds.

But at night

the world stands its ground alone,

and I

walk away from it

over the depths of my memory.

*

הַשָּׁמַיִם כְּבָר מֵתוּ. הָעֵץ
נוֹטֶה לָמוּת.
מִי יוֹדֵעַ, אוּלַי רַק הָאֶבֶן
תִּבָּדֵל לַחַיִּים,
תָּעִיד עָלֵינוּ
אִם לֹא יִרְצְחוּהָ
בּוֹנֵי כְּבִישִׁים בִּשְׁכוּנוֹת חֲדָשׁוֹת.

וּמִי יַאֲמִין שֶׁהָיָה לָנוּ שֵׁם
כָּתוּב בַּשָּׁמַיִם,
חָרוּט בִּקְלִפַּת הָעֵץ
וּבְלֵב הָאֶבֶן.
שֶׁהָיִינוּ
וְנָשַׁמְנוּ
וְגָסַסְנוּ
בָּעִיר הַזֹּאת.

*

The skies have already died. The tree

is dying.

Who knows, maybe only the stone

will be spared.

It will testify of us

if they don't kill it

the road-builders in new neighborhoods.

And who will believe we had a name

written in the sky,

inscribed in the tree's bark

and in the stone's heart.

That we lived

and breathed

and died

in this city.

*

זֶה מִכְּבָר אֵין אִישׁ מְחַכֶּה לִי שָׁם.
וְאִם אֵין יָם, הֲרֵי אֵין גַּם סְפִינָה.
הַדֶּרֶךְ קְצָרָה. הַחוּג צָמְצַם.
וּבְכֵן מָה?
עוֹד שָׁבוּעַ? עוֹד חֹדֶשׁ? עוֹד שָׁנָה?

אַחֲרֵי מוֹתִי עוֹד יִהְיֶה מַשֶּׁהוּ בָּעוֹלָם.
מִישֶׁהוּ יֹאהַב מִישֶׁהוּ, מִישֶׁהוּ יִשְׂנָא.
הַדֶּרֶךְ קְצָרָה. הַחֶשְׁבּוֹן לֹא הָשְׁלַם.
וּבְכֵן מָה?
עוֹד שָׁבוּעַ? עוֹד חֹדֶשׁ? עוֹד שָׁנָה?

הַטַּל נוֹפֵל. עֶרֶב צוֹנֵן עַל פָּנַי.
עַל פָּרָשַׁת הַדְּרָכִים הַקְּרוֹבָה אוֹתָהּ תַּחֲנָה.
מָחָר אֲנִי אֶתְעוֹרֵר וְאֶפְקַח אֶת עֵינַי –
אֱלֹהִים אַדִּירִים,
עוֹד שָׁבוּעַ, עוֹד חֹדֶשׁ, עוֹד שָׁנָה

*

For a while now no one is waiting there for me.

And if there's no sea, then there's also no boat.

The road is short. The sphere contracts.

And so, what?

Another week? Another month? Another year?

After my death there will still be something in the world.

Someone will love someone. Someone will hate.

The road is short. The account incomplete.

And so, what?

Another week? Another month? Another year?

The dew falls. Evening is cool on my face.

The same station at the crossroads near-by.

Tomorrow I'll wake and open my eyes –

dear God,

another week, another month, another year

תְּשׁוּבָה

על סעיף בשאלון "לשם מה
נכתבים שירים ליריים בדורנו?"

וּמַה לַעֲשׂוֹת בַּסּוּסִים בַּמֵּאָה הָעֶשְׂרִים?

וּבָאַיָּלוֹת?

וּבָאֲבָנִים הַגְּדוֹלוֹת

שֶׁבְּהָרֵי יְרוּשָׁלַיִם?

ANSWER

> To the exam question "For what purpose
> are lyric poems written in our era?"

And what would we do with the horses in the twentieth century?

And with the does?

And with the large stones

in the Jerusalem hills?

עֲלֵי צַפְצָפָה לְבָנִים

א.

עֲלֵי צַפְצָפָה לְבָנִים
מוּאָרִים עַל שְׁחוֹר הָאֵלֶם
וְכָל הַצִּפֳּרִים שׁוֹתְקוֹת
אֶת שְׁעוֹת הָעֶרֶב.
אֵיךְ הִצְלַחְתְּ
לִמְצוֹא לָךְ מִקְלָט
בְּאִי שֶׁאֵין בּוֹ
אֲפִלּוּ חֲלוֹם אֶחָד?

WHITE POPLAR LEAVES

I.

White poplar leaves

illuminated in the dark hush

and all the birds keeping

the evening hours quiet.

How did you manage

to find refuge for yourself

on an island that has not

even a single dream?

ב.

בִּשְׁתִיקָה מְזֻקֶּקֶת
רֵיקָה
הַשֵּׁם שֶׁצִּלְצֵל לַשָּׁוְא.
בִּשְׁתִיקָה מְנֻתֶּקֶת
דְּבוּקָה
בַּשֵּׁם הָאֶחָד.
בִּשְׁתִיקַת הַזְּכוּכִית
הַדַּקָּה עַד הַשֶּׁבֶר
הַשֵּׁם הָאֶחָד בִּשְׁתִיקָה
הוֹלֵךְ וְגוֹבֵר.

2.

In a purified silence

empty

is the name that sounded in vain.

In an isolated silence

cleaving

to the one name.

In silence of the glass

thin to near-breaking

the one name in silence

grows and grows.

ג.

שָׁלוֹם לִי, שָׁלוֹם לִי

וְאַל תִּתְפַּלֵּל לִשְׁלוֹמִי –

שָׁלוֹם לִי, שָׁלוֹם לִי

וְאַל תִּשְׁאַל בִּשְׁבִיל מִי –

אֲנִי אֲבוּדָה בְּשַׁלְוָה עֲמֻקָּה

אָזְנַי אֲטוּמוֹת

וּפָנַי

צָפוֹת עַל פְּנֵי הַשְּׁתִיקָה.

3.

Farewell to me, farewell

and do not pray for my well-being –

farewell to me, farewell

and do not ask for whom –

I am lost in a deep peace

my ears are sealed

and my face

floats on the surface of silence.

*

מָחָר אֲנִי אָמוּת

אַתֶּם תִּרְאוּ מָחָר

אֶת שֶׁהָיוּ עֵינַי

אֶת שֶׁהָיוּ פָּנַי.

לְעֵת מָחָר אַתֶּם

בָּאִים עַל סַף בֵּיתִי

לַחְלֹק אֶת הַכָּבוֹד

וּלְחַלֵּק שָׁלָל.

מָחָר יִהְיֶה הַכֹּל

לָכֶם וְשֶׁלָּכֶם.

מָחָר אַתֶּם צוֹדְקִים

בְּכָל אֲשֶׁר תֹּאמְרוּ.

אֲבָל הַיּוֹם אֲנִי

עוֹמֶדֶת עַל הַסַּף

וְאֶעֱבוֹר גְּבוּלִי

וְאֵין מַסִּיג אוֹתוֹ.

*

Tomorrow I will die.

Tomorrow you will see

what was my face

what were my eyes.

When tomorrow arrives you

will come to my doorstep

to pay last respects

and divide up the spoils.

Tomorrow all will be

yours and for you.

Tomorrow you are right

in everything you say.

But today I

stand at the threshold

and I'll cross over my border

and none may trespass.

*

וְזֶה יִהְיֶה הַדִּין

וְכָךְ יִהְיֶה הַדִּין,

וְאָז בְּיוֹם הַדִּין

יִהְיֶה צִדּוּק הַדִּין.

וְאָנוּ לֹא נֵדַע

וְאָנוּ לֹא נָבִין

וְנַעֲמוֹד אִלְּמִים

בִּפְנֵי צִדּוּק הַדִּין.

וְזֶה יִהְיֶה הַדִּין.

וְהַמֵּתִים בַּדִּין,

הֵם הָעֵדִים בַּדִּין,

כָּל הַמֵּתִים מֵאָז

וְהַמֵּתִים עַכְשָׁו.

*

And this will be the judgment
and thus will be the judgment,
and on the day of judgment
will be vindication of the judgment.

And we will not know
and we'll not understand
and we'll stand mute
before vindication of the judgment.
And this will be the judgment.

And those who die by judgment,
they're the lawful witnesses,
all who died since then
and those who die now.

הֵם מְעִידִים בַּדִּין

וְעֵדוּתָם אֱמֶת.

כִּי הֵם וְהַחַיִּים

כִּי הֵם צִדּוּק הַדִּין.

וְזֶה יִהְיֶה הַדִּין.

They attest by law of judgment

and their testimony is true.

For they and the living

are vindication of the judgment.

And this will be the judgment.

AFTERWORD
TO THE ORIGINAL HEBREW COLLECTION
by Tuvia Ruebner

Very few of the poems collected here have previously been published in journals or newspapers. Most of them were gleaned from notebooks and scattered papers which were found in the poet's house after her death. The last two poems in this collection were written by Lea Goldberg in the hospital in the very last days of her life.

Goldberg's notebooks included different versions of poems or poem-fragments, and it was up to me to decide which to print. The poems are not in chronological order. There were very few dates on the manuscript poems.

There is no knowing whether Lea Goldberg would have included in book-form all the poems she published when she was still alive. She did not always include in her published books all the poems she had published in individual fashion previously. And she, who aspired toward a degree of perfection, so much so that she often felt it necessary to illuminate a poetic subject from various perspectives and would include only isolated poems in her poetic series, would have undoubtedly omitted the poetic pieces I have collected here under the title "Fragments." I include them here in her memory. In my opinion, these poems clearly express a poetic idea, though its development may not be complete; in them unfolds what one sees also in the more formally articulated poem: the individual's experience as it evolves and is transformed through language. In addition, one feels in a powerful way the unmediated touch of these poems.

This collection does not include all the poems found in the notebooks; these are forthcoming in *The Collected Poems of Lea Goldberg*, which Sifriat Poalim is laboring now to publish.

My deepest gratitude is owed to Mrs. Yehudit Preiss; it is her active aid alone that made this book possible.

(1971)

In the Hebrew original, these remarks by Ruebner appear untitled and at the back of the collection. The now-canonical 3-volume *The Collected Poems of Lea Goldberg*, edited by Ruebner, was published in 1973. Yehudit Preiss was Goldberg's longstanding secretary.

NOTES

Tuvia Ruebner included fifty-nine poems in the collection – the number of years that Goldberg lived (Goldberg passed away four months short of her fifty-ninth birthday).

Biblical citations in these notes are from the Jewish Publication Society (JPS) translation unless otherwise indicated.

"A young poet suddenly falls silent"
The phrase "the best in a poem is its lie" (*meitav hashir kezavo*) is from Andalusian Hebrew poet Moses ibn Ezra (ca. 1055–after 1138), one of the preeminent poets of the Golden Age of medieval Hebrew poetry. Ibn Ezra makes this full assertion in his Arabic prose work *The Book of Discussion and Remembrance* (*Kitaab al Muhaadara wa-al-Mudhaakara*), a book translated into Hebrew by Ben Zion Halper and published under the title *Shirat Yisrael* in 1924 (Leipzig: Abraham Yosef Shtibel). The phrase "the best in a poem is its lie" was common parlance in Hebrew literary circles following that publication. See Peter Cole's *The Dream of the Poem: Hebrew Poetry from Muslim and Christian Spain 950–1492* (Princeton, NJ: Princeton University Press, 2007). For an extended discussion of the phrase and its various interpretations, see Dan Pagis' *Secular Poetry and Poetic Theory: Moses ibn Ezra and His Contemporaries* (Jerusalem: Mossad Bialik, 1970) 46-50 [Hebrew]. See also the discussion on pages xx–xxii in this collection.

It bears noting that Goldberg slightly changes the original phrase: *meitav hashir kezavo* becomes in Goldberg's poem *meitav hashir / shehu kezavo* – which would be rendered literally as "…in fear / of the best in a poem / **which is** its lie."

This poem stands as an epigraph poem in the original Hebrew collection, a placement and poetic function emulated here.

"And the poem I did not write"
Line 10: This line would be rendered literally as "Come descend to me, **Daughter of the Gods**" (*bat ha'elim* / בת האלים). The nine Muses of Greek mythology were, of course, the daughters of the gods Zeus and Mnemosyne (Memory). Goldberg is utilizing – and also subverting by naming the poetic composition a "game" – the traditional epic invocation of the Muse. The phrase *bat ha'elim* evokes also the collocation *bat-kol* – a divine voice. Finally, *bat ha'elim* may also be alluding to the distinctive biblical phrase *benei elim* – "sons of the gods." Cf. Psalms 29:1.

The colloquial Hebrew word for "muse" – *musa* / מוסה – is, like its English counterpart, lifted directly from the Greek original *mousa*.

"In everything there is at least an eighth part"
Line 3: The phrase *tamir vesha'anan*, translated here as "secret and carefree," evokes in its lexis and rhythm a familiar epithet for God: *Hahu tamir vene'elam* – "He who is hidden and unknown."

FRAGMENTS
The first two poems in this series are published here for the first time in Hebrew as in English. In the Hebrew original of "Fragments" – a title that Ruebner chose for this series – two poems that were in fact not by Goldberg were mistakenly included. These poems, found unattributed among Goldberg's papers, were later discovered to be by the poet Shlomo Zucker. Two poetic fragments from the Goldberg archives – "The distance between me and she in the poem" and "A person rises from his sleep" – were chosen to be included in place of the Zucker poems. Ruebner gave his approval to the choice of alternative fragments and the change to the original collection.

"The distance between me and the poem's she"
The second line-break in the English rendering has been placed differently from its Hebrew counterpart, in order to maintain the original poem's visual presentation.

On the Mount of Olives
Final line: The simple collocation *bamakom hazeh* – "in this place" – is used in various biblical passages, and evokes the sanctity of a place. See in particular Jacob's dream of the ascending and descending angels, which ends thus: "And Jacob awaked out of his sleep, and he said: 'Surely the Lord is in this place [*bamakom hazeh*]; and I knew it not.' And he was afraid, and he said: 'How full of awe is this place [*bamakom hazeh*]. This is none other than the house of God and this is the gate of heaven'" (Genesis 28:16-17).

Jerusalem, Earthly and Divine
The concept of *Yerushalyim shel mata vema'alah* ("Jerusalem, Earthly and Divine" – literally "Jerusalem of below and of above") conveys the rabbinic belief that Jerusalem was built in two parallel spheres: the spiritual realm (Heavenly Jerusalem) and the physical realm (Earthly Jerusalem). The term is used in the Babylonian

Talmud, Ta'anit 5a, where, in an exchange between two rabbis, one says to the other that "The Holy One, blessed be He, proclaimed: 'I will not come into the upper Jerusalem (*Yerushalayim shel ma'alah*) until I enter the lower Jerusalem (*Yerushalayim shel mata*).'"

Section 1 – Lines 3 & 4: Biblical translations of the Hebrew words *dardar* and *chochim* are more commonly, though not invariably, rendered as "thistles" and "thorns" respectively. See, for example, Genesis 3:18 – "Thorns also and **thistles** [*dardar*] shall it bring forth to thee" and conversely Song of Songs 2:2 – "As a lily among **thorns** [*chochim*], so is my love among the daughters." I have inverted these two renderings in order to achieve the more musically appealing image of "thorn jewels."

Section 2 – Lines 8–9: "David, King of Israel / lives on forever" is a popular Hebrew song – often sung by children – originating in a passage from Babylonian Talmud, Rosh Hashanah 25a.

Section 3 – Line 12: The reference is to the city of Hebron, famous for its glass-blowers. The royal-blue glass produced in the city is its best-known product.
Line 14: A swallow in Hebrew is gendered female. This line would be rendered literally as "The swallow she has no nest."

"The clasp of sand and stone"
See note 19 on page xxvii for an elaboration of the translation choices made for the repeated phrase "the clasp of sand and stone."

"The day turned"
For the repeated phrase "the day turned" (*hayom panah*), cf. Jeremiah 6:4: "Alas for us, for the day is declining [*ki fanah hayom*], the shadows of evening grow long" (New Jewish Publication Society translation). The phrase *ki fanah yom* is repeated throughout the closing prayer service (*Ne'ilah*) of Yom Kippur, with an awareness that the day is ebbing and the metaphorical gates of life are about to be closed. (The פ is without a dagesh – a dot in its center – because it follows the long vowel of *ki* and is therefore pronounced as *fanah* instead of *panah*.)

Goldberg was clearly influenced by this phrase and prayer (*piyyut*, a liturgical poem); indeed, it appears elsewhere in her oeuvre, from the earliest poems (for example, in the untitled "The world is heavy on our eyelids," the final poem in her first collection *The Green-Eyed Stalk*) to her uncollected work (for example, section 2 of the stunning four-part poetic series *Ne'ilah*. For English renderings of these poems, see *Lea Goldberg: Selected Poetry and Drama*, pp. 47, 198–201). In addition, in her *Encounters with a Poet*, Goldberg's memoir about Avraham Ben Yitzhak (known as Sonne) – a pivotal figure and poet in modern Hebrew letters and an important person in Goldberg's life personally – she recalls Sonne's recitation of this *piyyut* thus:

> About the piyyut, and poetry of the Haskalah period…he would talk with great enthusiasm… He would recite the lines so beloved by him with great warmth and emotion, every word imbued with extra weight and truth. I have never before heard a person recite poetry as he did. And many still remember how he would recite "one of the most beautiful lyrical poems in Hebrew" – from the *Ne'ilah* prayer service of Yom Kippur:
>
> > Open for us a gate
> > at the hour the gate is sealed,
> > for the day has turned.

See Goldberg's *Encounters with a Poet* (Tel Aviv: Sifriat Poalim, 2009), p. 63 [Hebrew].

"My entire life summed up in that one moment –"
Line 2: The Hebrew original is built around the homonym of *keren*, which means both "light-ray" (*keren shel or*) and "antler" or "horn" (*keren hatzvi*). The collocation *keren hatzvi* is also an idiom for "a doubtful enterprise," as in the expression "שם כספו על קרן הצבי" (rendered literally as, "To put one's money on the deer's antler").

"There were questions"
Line 7: The possessive of "*its* sorrow" is female in the Hebrew original, referring back to the female gendered "land" or "sun" of the previous lines.

"The face of the waters"
Line 1: Cf. Genesis 1:2: "…and the spirit of God hovered over the face of the waters."
Line 2: Cf. Genesis 1:16: "And God made the two great lights: the greater light to rule the day, and the lesser light [*ma'or hakatan*] to rule the night; and the stars."
Line 3: The word *diber* / דִּבֶּר – rendered here as "the spoken word" – denotes speech, or the power of speech. Cf. Jeremiah 5:13: "And the prophets shall become wind, and the word [*hadiber*] is not in them "). See also The Gospel of John, 1:1: "In the beginning was the Word and the Word was with God and the Word was God" (KJV).

SONGS OF SPAIN
1. Passerby
Line 4: *negidei-hashir*, here rendered as "Princes of Song," is an allusion to the Andalusian Hebrew poet Shmu'el HaNagid (993–1056). The word *nagid* – which becomes *negid* in the possessive form – means, variously, governor, ruler, or prince.
Line 5: The allusion here is to the thousands who were burned at the stake during the Spanish Inquisition.

4. With Glory and In Poverty
The second stanza of this poem casts Granada in two contrasting biblical images of Jerusalem: the abandoned, ash-covered and ruined city of the Book of Lamentations and the beautifully gardened city of Song of Songs. Indeed, in the third and fourth lines of the stanza, Goldberg inserts the stones and ash of Lamentations – *hayoshevet be'afar uva'even / aturat ganim* – into the well-known verse from Song of Songs that describes Jerusalem as *hayoshevet baganim* ("Thou [female] that dwellest in the gardens," Song of Songs 8:13). The word "city" is gendered female in Hebrew.

5. I Talk To You
The Hebrew original of this poem is built around the very prominent end-rhyme of the *hireq* vowel sound (long e). Of the eighteen lines, thirteen end with a *hireq*: *leshoni, ivri, tizkeri, leshoni, tizkeri* (stanza 1: lines 1, 3-4, 6-7); *shiri, ani, ovri,* (stanza 2: lines 1-3); *ka'ari, ovri, nokhri, ani, ovri* (stanza 3: lines 1-5). The English rendering has attempted to compensate for this lost rhyme with alternative sound patterns.

SMALL POEMS
2. At the Small Station
Line 1: Cf. Psalm 121:1: "…I will lift up mine eyes unto the mountains: from whence shall my help come?"

3. All of Night's Stars
Line 2: Cf. Psalm 115:16: "The heavens belong to the Lord, but the earth He gave over to man" (New Jewish Publication Society translation). This phrase is incorporated into the *Hallel* service (prayers of praise), recited during morning prayers at the beginning of a new month and on other festival days.

"The hills today are like shadows of hills"
See notes 29–32 on pages xxx–xxxi for further explication of this poem and of

translation choices made. In the poem's first line, Goldberg is referencing and subverting the Hebrew idiom *ra'ah et tsel heharim keharim* – "he saw the shadow of hills as hills" (meaning, he is "making mountains out of molehills").

Nightmare
Lines 6, 11 & 17: The paradoxical refrain "Wake me. I'm not asleep" evokes Song of Songs 5:2: "I sleep, but my heart is awake; It is the voice of my beloved! He knocks, saying, 'Open for me, my sister, my love'" (New King James Version). Goldberg utilizes this same verse most pronouncedly in the second section of her well-known "Songs of My Beloved Land" (*Shirei Eretz Ahavati*) and rewrites the verse in a later poem, "Lovers on the Beach." For English versions of both, see *Lea Goldberg: Selected Poetry and Drama*, pp. 108–10, 121–22.
Line 16: The words *emet ve'emunah*, rendered here as "Truth and faith," are the first words of a blessing spoken immediately after the Shema is recited in the evening (*ma'ariv*) prayer service. The blessing is an affirmation of the truthfulness of all that has been previously spoken.

"The swallows"
Line 11: For *nishkefah*, of the phrase *lo nishkefah* – rendered here as "unseen" – cf. Judges 5:28: "בעד החלון נִשְׁקְפָה ותיבב אם סיסרא, בעד האשנב: מדוע בשש רכבו לבוא..." ("The mother of Sisera looked through the window, and cried out through the lattice, 'Why is his chariot so long in coming?...'" NKJV).
Line 12: The "old city" may, in fact, be the Old City of Jerusalem. As Hebrew has no capital letters, the phrase remains open to multiple readings.

Upon Reading Dante
Section 1: The poem's epigraph – from Dante's *Inferno*, Canto v, line 138 – reads thus in the original: "quel giorno più non vi leggemmo avante" ("that day we read no further"). The footnote here and in section 2 are Ruebner's. Emanuel Olsbanger's translations into Hebrew of the Italian are replaced in the English footnotes with Allen Mandelbaum's English renderings of the same.

Section 2: The poem's first line is a translation of the Italian epigraph.

Section 3, Line 1: The allusion is to David's Lament for Saul and Jonathan. Cf. 2 Samuel 1:23: "Saul and Jonathan, the lovely and the pleasant in their lives, even in their death they were not divided...." See Goldberg's "The Lament of Odysseus" (*Lea Goldberg: Selected Poetry and Drama*, p. 73, and note on the poem on pp. 210–11) for a more extensive use of David's Lament.

On the Dangers of Smoking

Line 7: The literal rendering of the opening phrase in the Hebrew original is "Wisdom's fence?" The clear reference, resonant in the Hebrew, is to the saying "Silence is a fence around wisdom," or, in its original brevity and syntax: "Wisdom's fence, silence" (Ethics of the Fathers 3, end of verse 13). I have added the word "silence" to my translation, to open an avenue to the poem's allusion, otherwise inaccessible in the English.

"You have no right to pardon in the world"

Line 2: This line may be an allusion to, and subtle inversion of, Ethics of Fathers 3:15: "All is foreseen, and freedom of choice is given."

Lines 3–4: These lines echo the words "My creations drown in the sea, and you speak poetry" ("מעשי ידי טובעים בים ואתם אומרים שירה"). According to this midrash, when the Egyptians were drowning in the Red Sea that had closed on them, the angels began to sing songs of triumph and revenge; God spoke then these words, forbidding their joy. See Babylonian Talmud, Megillah 10a.

"We wrote words like:"

Lines 4 & 8: The phrase *baruch dayan ha'emet* – Blessed is the True Judge – is spoken upon hearing of a death. The full prayer, recited by the bereaved when his/her garment is ripped in the funeral ritual of *kriyah* (literally "rending"), is "ברוך אתה אדני אלוהינו מלך העולם ברוך דיין האמת" (*baruch ata adonai eloheynu melekh ha'olam baruch dayan ha'emet*). Goldberg offers the phrase without the definite article – *baruch dayan emet* – which reflects a more colloquial, but not non-normative, usage.

Illness

Final line: For *al penei tehom*, rendered here as "over the depths of," cf. Genesis 1:2: "והארץ היתה תהו ובהו, וחושך על פני התהום" ("Now the earth was unformed and void, and darkness was upon the face of the deep").

"The skies have already died. The tree"

Line 4: The expression *tibadel lechayim*, here rendered simply as "will be spared," means literally "set apart for life." The phrase is spoken to wish someone a long life, particularly after the dead have been mentioned.

"For a while now no one is waiting there for me."

Line 3: The phrase *hachug tsumtsam* – rendered as "The sphere contracts" – evokes the Kabbalistic notion of *tsimtsum*, whereby creation began with the infinite divine spirit contracting itself to make room for the finite world to come into being. The verb form in the Hebrew is passive ("was contracted").

Answer
Line 2: The does in this line and the repeated questions of the text echo Goldberg's iconic book of children's verse: *Mah Osot HaAyalot?* (*What Do the Does Do?*). The collection was first published in 1949, with illustrations by Aryeh Navon, and has since become a mainstay in Hebrew children's literature. The first poem in the collection, the eponymous "Mah Osot HaAyalot," was put to music and is for many the book's most beloved poem.

White Poplar Leaves
Section 1, Lines 3–4: Goldberg has used a non-grammatical formulation by transforming the verb *shotek* or *shotkim* – "keeping quiet" – into a transitive verb, with the direct object being "the evening hours" of the following line. I have tried to recreate some of the original dissonance of these two lines in the English.
Line 5: The addressee is female.

Section 2: The repeated "the name" – *HaShem* – is another title for God.

Section 3, Lines 1 & 3: Literally, "Peace unto me."

"Tomorrow I will die" and "And This will be the judgment"
These two poems – Goldberg's last – were written in the hospital, a few days before her death.

"Tomorrow I will die"
The "you" in this poem is plural.

Lines 7 & 8: The verbs of these two lines – *lachalok* (rendered as "to divide [the spoils]") and *lichalek* (rendered as "to pay [respect]") – are from the same root of *het, lamed, kuf,* meaning to divide or impart.

"And this will be the judgment"
Line 3: Yom HaDin – the Day of Judgment – is one of the names of Rosh Hashanah.
Lines 4, 8 & 17: The phrase *tsiduk hadin*, here rendered as "vindication of the judgment," is a reference to the prayer known by that name, spoken by mourners at the graveside immediately after the grave has been filled with earth. The prayer affirms acceptance of God's decree, and the righteousness and compassion of all God's doings, including the death of a beloved.
Line 16: The word for "the living" – *hachayim* – means also "life."
This poem is eighteen lines long; the number eighteen, *chai* in gematria, signifies life.

BOOKS BY LEA GOLDBERG*

POETRY

Smoke Rings [טבעות עשן]   1935

The Green-Eyed Stalk [שבולת ירקת העין]   1939

Songs in the Villages [שיר בכפרים: מחרוזת שירי עם]   1942

From My Old Home [מביתי הישן]   1944

On the Flowering [על הפריחה]   1948

Samson's Love [אהבת שמשון]   1952

Lightning in the Morning [ברק בבוקר]   1955

Early and Later: Selected Poems [מקדם ומאחר: מבחר שירים]   1959

With This Night [עם הלילה הזה]   1964

Selected Poems [ילקוט שירים]   1970

The Remains of Life [שארית החיים: שירים רשומים מן העזבון]   1971

Collected Poems [3 vols.] [שירים]   1973; rev. ed. 1986

Small [זוטא]   1981

Poems [שירים]   1986

You Will Walk in the Fields (poems & songs) [את תלכי בשדה]   1989

Selected Poems [מבחר שירים]   1989

In My Beloved Country [בארץ אהבתי: מבחר שירי אהבה]   1997

Love and Gold Poems: The Sonnets of Lea Goldberg
 [שירי אהב"ה וזה"ב: הסונטות של לאה גולדברג]   2008

Urban Poems: Unpublished Poems by Lea Goldberg Inspired by Woodcuts by Frans Masereel [שיר | עיר: צרור שירים גנוזים מאת לאה גולדברג לחיתוכי עץ מאת פרנץ מזרל]   2012

---

* This bibliography does not include the numerous volumes of Goldberg's books for children, or her many books of translated literature and literary criticism.

PLAYS

The Lady of the Castle (*A Dramatic Episode in Three Acts*)
[בעלת הארמון: אפיזודה דרמטית בשלוש מערכות]   1956; 1974; 2014

Plays [מחזות]   1979

Plays: Known & From the Archives [מחזות: גנוזים וידועים]   2011

PROSE

Letters from an Imaginary Journey (novel) [מכתבים מנסיעה מדומה]   1937; 1982; 2007

And This Is the Light (novel) [והוא האור]   1946: 1994; 2005

Encounter With a Poet (*On Avraham Ben-Yizthak Sonne*)
[פגישה עם משורר: (על אברהם בן-יצחק סונה)]   1952; 1988; 2009

Lea Goldberg: The Complete Short Stories [לאה גולדברג: כל הסיפורים]   2009

Losses (novel) [אבדות] Composed in 1937, published in 2010

BOOKS IN ENGLISH TRANSLATION

Selected Poems, translated and introduced by Robert Friend; foreword by Yehuda Amichai; afterword by Gershom Scholem (1976)

On the Blossoming, translated with an afterword by Miriam Billig Sivan (1992)

Lea Goldberg: Selected Poetry and Drama, poetry translated and introduced by Rachel Tzvia Back, play translated by T. Carmi (2005)

With This Night, translated by Annie Kantar (2011)

And This Is the Light, translated by Barbara Harshav (2011)

BOOKS BY RACHEL TZVIA BACK

POETRY

Litany   1995

Azimuth   2001

The Buffalo Poems   2003

On Ruins & Return: Poems 1999–2005   2007

A Messenger Comes (Elegies)   2012

TRANSLATIONS

Lea Goldberg: Selected Poetry and Drama (play translation by T. Carmi)   2005

Night, Morning: Selected Poems of Hamutal Bar-Yosef   2008

With an Iron Pen: Twenty Years of Hebrew Protest Poetry   2009

In the Illuminated Dark: Selected Poems of Tuvia Ruebner   2014

CRITICAL WORK

Led by Language: the Poetry & Poetics of Susan Howe   2002